CRUISING PAST SEVENTY

IT'S NOT ONLY ABOUT OUTER JOURNEYS.
IT'S ALSO ABOUT INNER ONES.

§

Carolina Esguerra Colborn

ISBN: 979-8-693773-92-9

Cover by Dennis Siochi Aberion
Book interior designed by YouTbooks.com

FOREWORD

I first "met" Carol in the fall of 2019, when she submitted a trial article and a collection of original photography for publication on *TravelAwaits*. I vividly remember a photo of her and her husband, Bill, standing in front of I. M. Pei's Louvre Pyramid, which we published as the cover photo for her submission "Lessons From The Road: It's All About Attitude." Carol's wearing a beautiful, vibrantly colored scarf and a big smile. Bill has on a backpack and a ballcap. They hold one another in a gentle embrace. Carol has a spritely look about her that says *joie de vivre*.

That zest for life and the journey, both within and without, is exactly what you'll find in this book. Carol's writing has satisfied both the daydreamer and the anthropologist in me, and I know it will speak to those parts, and others, in anyone who chooses to cruise through its pages. She has a way of illuminating the little details with profound straightforwardness while also highlighting the threads that pull the big picture together. She invites you to get in touch with that part of yourself that longs to hit the road or jet set across the pond, and, in this book, suggests that the desire to experience faraway places and life on the road is about accumulating the experiences required to deepen and enrich our inner lives.

These journeys will look different for everyone, and Carol's certainly captivate. As I got to know her through her *TravelAwaits* submissions, I could hardly believe someone had the tenacity, endurance, and open-heartedness to finish a corporate career in the Philippines, emigrate to the United States, find new love, and hit the road in a massive Class A RV for an eight-year honeymoon. Carol and I have four decades between us, and sometimes I have trouble keeping up with her energy!

Carol's sense of humor makes her accounts of her travels that much more delightful to read. When the *TravelAwaits* team received her "Shifting Gears" submission, in which she details how and why her approach to travel changed from her sixties to her seventies, we shared in the joy and laughter of encountering the word sexygenarian for the first time. Carol explained that she coined this term as a substitute for sexagenarian "to make it more exciting." Rest assured that elements of "Shifting Gears" have made their way into *Cruising Past Seventy* for your enjoyment.

Like her sense of humor, Carol's self-awareness is refreshing. I love her accounts of pushing the limits of their itineraries (and maybe Bill's patience!), pulling all-nighters to see the Northern Lights, and "Meddling in the UK"—a section of Chapter 4 that details her spirited interactions with her daughter and son-in-law as they planned their Scottish Highlands wedding and hosted her in their home in Newcastle-upon-Tyne.

The Alaska girl in me (I was born in Juneau and spent my young childhood outside of Anchorage in Eagle River) also appreciates Carol's reflections on the Last Frontier. I've been brought to tears by her accounts of what becoming an American has meant for her— perhaps because I've worked with refugees in St. Louis for twelve years, including a three-year stint as an adult ESL teacher, though I've been equally moved by her stories of encountering Filipino food and sailors in Mexico and appreciating structures of historical and religious significance around the U.S. and the world.

The fact that Carol finished *Cruising Past Seventy* while on lockdown in Arizona will not be lost on anyone, and there's something very therapeutic about her writing, especially today. Carol proves that experiencing the wonder of a child is not necessarily lost with age but can be augmented by wisdom. This experience of wonder, wisdom, levity, and inspiration is her gift to her readers. Get comfy and enjoy!

Linsey D. D. Stevens
Copy & Developmental Editor
In-House Editorial Strategist, *TravelAwaits*

PREFACE

In 2004 I retired early and migrated to America, weighing just 101 pounds after burning out from a jet-setting business life in Manila. I needed a huge change and wanted to find time to "cook a little, teach a little, travel a little, write a little, and love a little." And I did, especially the last one, and married a businessman who took me RVing all over North America. I ended up writing my first travel book about those eight years. He wholeheartedly supported the making of my book, *Carolina: Cruising to an American Dream*, but this time around, he complained that I had forgotten about that operative term, "a little." I told him that he would not like a bored Carol and the stress is not the like the one that led me to retire early. It's called positive stress.

When my husband and I were approaching our seventies, we moved beyond fulltime RVing and settled in a home in Phoenix. I also rebranded the blog that I started when we began the odyssey to *Cruising Past 70*. The shift included writing more about inner journeys, reflections about my travels beyond just the accounting of the outer ones. It had been five years since I published the first book in 2015. I also found almost the same number of posts I had written from the time of that first book's writing. I was ready for another book, I thought. This time, however, I became more selective. I zeroed in on those posts that elicited at least 1,000 views (some had 10,000, others had more than 30,000).

I considered them the best-loved and most widely-read posts and assumed that they became such because they were an excellent invitation to visit a place, answered a reader's question (s), or inspired a new pathway (s). I thought that it would be good to share them with those of you who have been retired, just retired or are thinking of retiring. For those who have read those posts, you may love having them all in one book. Thus, despite my husband's objections, I proceeded with the project.

Unfortunately, a macular hole developed in my right eye in September of last year. After the vitrectomy, I had to go through a somewhat difficult recovery, and then the healing happened slowly. Months later, my vision stabilized but it did not return to what it was before. I couldn't finish the book. I needed a lot more time. When coronavirus upended all our lives and was declared a pandemic in March, we cut short our Mexican vacation. The ensuing self-quarantine and lockdown gave me all the time I needed to complete a first draft. In fact, it also gave six of my friends the time to read it and give me the feedback I needed to complete the book in the next three months.

By December last year, I also had become a regular bimonthly writer for an online travel magazine, *TravelAwaits*. I have asked their permission to include in this book six of the original twenty-three articles I wrote for them. In fact, the Editorial Strategist wrote this book's Foreword. After updating and polishing each of the posts and articles I have included, they organize well into the three thematic parts of this book.

This book has become so relevant for the times. Now that we are not able to travel as much as we want, blending our outer journeys with the inner journeys that come as a result of them should better feed our wanderlust. This is how, even if we are forced to travel less, especially as we advance in years, our life becomes enriched. Because that's when we see benefits of travel that are deep and long-lasting. They are the lessons learned, changes made, and insights gained.

Carol E Colton

Author

TABLE OF CONTENTS

INTRODUCTION   15

A Traveler's Soul   15

Getting Older   17

Shifting Gears   19

PART 1: LESSONS LEARNED   23

Chapter 1:   The Pros and Cons of Making the RV Your Home   25

Chapter 2:   Buying Our New Home   31

Chapter 3:   Camping around America   35

Chapter 4:   An Epic Alaska Road Trip in Our Own RV   41

Chapter 5:   Finding Christmas on Treasure Island   49

Chapter 6:   Turning Wounds into Wisdom   55

Chapter 7:   Operationalizing Fulltime RVing   63

Chapter 8:   Another Epic Road Trip to Alaska in a Rented RV   69

Chapter 9:   Discovering the Secrets of the Manhattan Project   77

Chapter 10: Utilizing Technology on the Go   85

Chapter 11: Traveling Light in an RV   91

Chapter 12: Overhauling Carol   97

Chapter 13: Looking for a Base in Arizona   103

Chapter 14: What We Learned from Eight Years of RVing   113

Chapter 15: Discovering America, the Beautiful   119

PART 2: CHANGES MADE   127

Chapter 1:   Finally, Becoming a Wife   131

           v. Reliving WWII in the Philippines   137

Chapter 2:   More than a Writer   143

           v. Taking an Interest in Photography   147

Chapter 3:   A Better Wanderer   151

           v. Accidental Pilgrims   154

Chapter 4:   Finally, a Mother   161

           v1. Meddling in the UK   162

           v2. A Mother's Day Getaway   165

           v3. In My Daughter's Eyes   169

Chapter 5:   And Then a Promotion   173

           v1. A Nanny in London   174

           v2. Just Keeping Him Company   177

           v3. Through Her Millennial Eyes   180

Chapter 6: Finding a Second Home   187

    v1. Becoming an American   188

    v2. Finding Our Place in the Sun   190

Chapter 7: Rekindling the Filipino   199

    v1. Manong and His Jeepney   203

Chapter 8: Finding a Third Home   209

    v1. My First Impressions of Mexico   210

    v2. Filipino-Mexican Parallels   215

Chapter 9: Turning Global   219

    v1. Why I Will Go Back to the UK in a Jiffy   220

    v2. Australia, the New A-Dream   223

PART 3: INSIGHTS GAINED   231

Chapter 1: It's All about Attitude   235

Chapter 2: Travel Mishaps and How to View Them   241

Chapter 3: Falling Ill When You Least Expect It   245

Chapter 4: You Can Relive First Time Thrills   251

Chapter 5: You Must Get Used to Change   257

Chapter 6: Beautiful People on the Road   263

Chapter 7: Traveling with Friends or with Your Partner   269

Chapter 8: Which Season is the Best Time to Travel   275

Chapter 9:   Are a Few Hours Enough?   279

Chapter 10: Brand New or Old Favorite?   285

Chapter 11: Chasing a Photograph   289

Chapter 12: Every Traveler Needs a Great
                     Transportation Infrastructure   293

Chapter 13: Discovering Really Great Food   299

Chapter 14: There is No Need to Break Rules   305

Chapter 15: We Dared Go to Tunisia   309

Chapter 16: We Were Warned but We Drove Anyway   315

Chapter 17: Travel in the Time of Coronavirus   321

Chapter 18: On Keeping Fit   327

CONCLUSION   335

Shifting My Approach to Travel   335

Cruising to the End   338

ACKNOWLEDGMENTS   341

ABOUT THE AUTHOR   345

INTRODUCTION

A TRAVELER'S SOUL

When I turned seventy, family and friends could not understand why I was still constantly on the go. They said it was already way past mandatory retirement age. Not nowadays, I push back. Some people still work in their seventies; I still choose to travel. My husband Bill does, too. He's turning seventy-seven in March and it's great that he loves to drive because I can't. And road trips are so much more appropriate in times like these.

What pushes me to keep going? Sixteen years ago, I retired from jobs that had me going to various countries first to learn the various facets of information technology, and later to learn how they pioneered the IT applications we needed to replicate in the Philippines— interbank ATM transactions, automation of the internal revenue system, electoral automation, and even e-procurement. I was thrilled to get such awesome trips as parts of the jobs.

But they never were the kind of travel that touched my traveler's soul. I suspect that what drives me started much earlier than my corporate life. That was why, when I retired, something powerful was unleashed. When I was no longer confined to trips defined by jobs, my exploration of the world became unleashed. I literally began to travel all over the map.

One significant influence could have been my mother's journeys across the globe. She was sent everywhere, starting with winning a Philippine government scholarship to the US to study how the deaf were educated and how they were taught to speak. During her year-long grant, she wrote us letters. One of the most defining moments of my life was when she enclosed dry gold, yellow, orange and red maple leaves that had fallen from trees in autumn. I was fascinated. I thought, "I wonder if she can send us snow!" I was only eight.

But there was something more and now I remember what it might have been. My mother always insisted that I eat chicken wings. And she served them to us often in countless ways, as *adobo, nilaga, tinola, afritada, ginataan, inihaw, arroz caldo*, steak, barbeque, and, of course, fried. She believed like all the old folks back then that this would give anyone "wings with which to fly the world." I ate a ton.

Later I developed an intense liking for another part of the glorious chicken. Everybody loves Chinese food, I know; but I didn't develop much taste for *siopao, siomai,* egg rolls, Chinese fried rice, or congee. My favorite is something not many people know or even like. It is called "Phoenix Claws." (No wonder I was drawn to Phoenix, Arizona) It's a Chinese dish made from chicken feet. Yes, chicken feet that are fried, braised and simmered to perfection as tender, gelatinous and flavor-packed cartilage, skin, and bones. Trust me, if you can ever get over the mental hurdle, you will enjoy the best Chinese dish you will ever taste. I got over mine early on and have been hooked ever since. It is very hard and extremely time-consuming to make, so I order it every time I am at a dim sum place.

Chicken wings gave me reason to fly; chicken feet gave me reason to go on the road. Now you know why I was also drawn to RVing. In fact, my first book *Carolina: Cruising to an American Dream* is all about those eight years on the road. And I have not stopped eating those chicken dishes. That is why I may never stop traveling and perhaps that's the secret of my traveling soul.

GETTING OLDER

When I turned forty, I gasped, "On no, soon I will be old!" Well, it seemed to come sooner rather than later. Two years ago, I turned seventy. Now I say, "Oh no, I AM old!" But allow me to put "old" in perspective. The Filipina (female from the Philippines) lives on average, seventy-two years. But I have moved to America, where the average lifespan of a female is eighty-four. I left my stressful life in the Philippines and migrated to America in 2004. I am still very much alive and have added twelve more years to my life, just like that (if only it could be that simple).

17

But what does *average lifespan* actually mean? It means that in the years prior to reaching that number, your body will, as it is meant to do, probably begin to break down. We were in the middle of our RVing years when I turned sixty-two and I felt just like that. I had a case of recurring, invasive, and pervasive hives for two years; followed by strong bouts of acid reflux, heartburn, and other digestive problems. Then the inevitable happened: I had to have my cataracts removed. Then a macular hole developed on my right eye.

Besides these physiological changes, however, the psychological ones were even more dramatic. The main thing that changed is a mellowing and balancing of my life. I used to be driven by huge goals—studying to finish my doctorate, working for leading pioneers in information technology in my country, contributing to industry and national goals, and singlehandedly bringing up three children, all at the same time.

In my first book, *Carolina: Cruising*, I wrote: "As a career-driven working single parent to three daughters, I was completely burned out by the time I turned fifty. I had to get out of the fast lane. Right on cue, the ghost of my American dream reappeared. It was different though, no longer to make a fortune or a name but to find a new lifestyle, the exact opposite of the one I had been trying to prop up. I wanted time to cook a little, teach a little, travel a little, write a little, and love a little. The Philippines was not the place where that last one could happen. At my age, all the good ones had been taken." After fifteen years of retirement in America, I am pleased to report that all five modest goals have been accomplished.

The relationships I keep have become simpler, too. Most of my time is spent with my beloved Bill. Everybody who knows him says he is an angel; single Filipina friends ask me if by chance he has a brother. My own children side with him when we have an argument.

I am so lucky that he takes care of me. In turn, I do take care of him, too. This CEO has learned how to be a wife.

Our children are also already all grown; the truth is that they do not need much from us anymore. And they gave us grandchildren who give us so much joy. Finally, there are family and friends, some who visit us, some whom we visit, and our neighbors who are the valued constants in our life. We also try to keep in touch with many others, even if just virtually. Arranging reunions with them has become a happy, regular activity.

Generally, I may be experiencing more health issues, but they come with less striving, more peace, and overall happiness. The last line in my first book underlines that main change from the corporate Carol. "My new calling card says it best. Carolina Esguerra Colborn: Wanderer, Writer, Wife." And now I simply add the description "older."

SHIFTING GEARS

The first year Bill and I had monumental milestones was 2008 when I turned a "sexygenarian" and we were married. In 2018, we celebrated our tenth wedding anniversary. It was also the year I became a "sensuagenarian" (I know, it isn't as sexy). Both were times when I said goodbye to the past and hello to the new years ahead. We always feel this way when the old year magically transforms into a new one at midnight on December 31. But when I turned seventy, it was different. It was an occasion of fever-pitch intensity.

It signaled a shifting of gears. Actually, we had prepared for this a year earlier. We sold our RV and completed getting settled in our new home at Viewpoint Golf Resort in Mesa, Arizona in 2017. And then we slowed our pace. In 2018, we did nineteen destinations in thirteen weeks. Even if we traveled five more weeks in 2019, it was just to ten destinations. We had upgraded to an all-inclusive twelve-week stay per year at any of El Cid's seven resorts in Mexico.

To save travel dollars, there were times in the past when I had flown thirty-six hours instead of eighteen, chosen cheaper lodging far from the city center instead of close to the sights, and eaten street or fast food instead of dining in style. But now that we are in our seventies, we are traveling less, going more slowly and more comfortably, even if we have to spend more.

I have even rebranded my blog as *Cruising Past 70* in anticipation of the shift. And my writing has changed. I started to pen more travel essays, not just travel diaries (records of what I did in a place or trip) or travel guides (information one must know about them). Instead, I began to write about why a place or a trip moved me. I began to share the inner journeys, the ones that were not so obvious. Of the almost 500 posts in the past ten years, 100+ are essays. All but a few of those were written in the past two years.

There must be something about turning seventy that heightens introspection. Maybe one reason is that an older brain and body can handle only so much, and we are forced to pause with increasing frequency. Maybe another is that having a partner encourages one to act much less on impulse, and we care about the other persons sometimes even more than ourselves, pausing and considering them before acting. Lastly, I have found that there's a decided benefit from not being always on the go. There's time and space to think and feel.

A travel essay begins with the traveler's realization that there is something regarding the place or journey truly worth writing about and sharing with others. It is not writing about what happened just for the purpose of keeping a record for future retrieval. It does not always have to be a big AHA! Moment; but it is an awakening nevertheless, however small. It requires that the writer be brave enough to reveal more, and share regardless of what others may say. As Bill and I have accumulated the years, it's good we have collected neither debt nor enemies, but memories of lessons learned, changes made, and insights gained.

This book, *Cruising Past Seventy*, is a compilation of the most-read of my blog posts and some of the best-loved articles I wrote for *TravelAwaits*, the online magazine I regularly write for nowadays. To be included here, the post had to have more than 1,000 page views. Some even reached as many as 30,000. I updated and polished each one, reflecting from the comments I had received. This introduction, for example, is a blending of three essays.

Part 1, "Lessons Learned," gives the highlights of our RVing years and zeroes in on lessons learned. I hope that it helps the reader realize that RVing is just another mode of travel; and that these lessons may be transferable not only to other modes but to travel in general, and maybe even to life.

Part 2, "Changes Made," is about the transformative power of travel. As the lessons piled up, big changes gradually happened. The facets of the new Carol—wanderer, writer, wife—have in fact increased to include becoming a mother, grandmother, American, Filipino-American, and a global citizen.

Part 3, "Insights Gained," consists of the reflections that crossed my mind, primarily after our trips, about common concerns of travelers. I hope you take away something of value from these insights.

Carolina: Cruising was my first attempt at writing a travel book. Back then, I thought the priority was to describe in detail every every place we visited. This book is a little different. I have tried to strike more of a balance, sharing more of what I think, feel, and value. I hope you like it.

PART 1

LESSONS LEARNED

§

"Like all great travelers, I have seen more than I remember
and remember more than I have seen."

—— BENJAMIN DISRAELI

At 8 PM on 8/8/08, Bill, 64 and I, nearly 60, started putting it all together. Our wedding was held on board *Champagne Lady*, cruising on Lake Union in Seattle, Washington. In what was the third for each of us, luckily we found the person with whom we could spend the rest of our lives. We'd found each other on the Net, of all places. The story was told in *Carolina: Cruising,* but many have asked me to write a full book on how to find a good lifetime partner on the Net.

A late-in-life marriage made our wedding even more mean-ingful. We wanted to focus on cruising along in life after years of hard work to provide for our families; so we chose a private cruise ship for the ceremony. And then our honeymoon almost became never-ending. With our fascination with the number eight, we made the RV our home for— of course— eight years. In effect, we "cruised" to a life together of cruising.

You may have noticed I use the word "cruise" a lot. The following definitions of the word resonate with us: 1) To travel about without necessarily a particular purpose or destination; 2) To drive at a constant speed that permits maximum operating efficiency for sustained travel; and 3) To travel at a moderately fast, easily controllable speed, such as cruising along the highway to enjoy the scenery. These closely define the cruising lifestyle that evolved for us after the wedding although I must admit we did not always stay true to these meanings, especially in the beginning. But it is now definitely the way we travel, past seventy.

From those RVing years, we learned our first lessons together; they comprised the appendices in my first book and some of the articles I wrote for *TravelAwaits*. Taken together, they are a glimpse into the RVing lifestyle we developed. I have updated them with the benefit of hindsight and comments I received on the original blog posts. I have separated the five most basic articles and put them together into a handy booklet, *Cruising in an RV. the basics you need to know,* which is now available in Amazon.

The rest is now Part 1 of this book. If you are not interested in RVing, you may wish to skip to Part 2. But even if you will not go RVing, you may be curious to see how some of the lessons apply to other modes of travel or life in general. If you are recently into or want to go RVing, especially since it is now an increasingly popular way to travel during the pandemic, this part may help you with the first things to know. If you are seasoned RVers, you may identify with many of our stories.

1

THE PROS AND CONS OF MAKING THE RV YOUR HOME

Our lifestyles were quite driven before we married and fully retired. Bill was keeping a small business in Seattle alive in a flagging economy after years of navigating the corporate jungle. In turn, I was juggling teaching at three institutions of higher learning in Seattle while babysitting my grandson after working for years in the Philippine corporate landscape. The RV cruising lifestyle was so refreshing after our highly stressful working lives.

At the time this pros-and-cons debate was going on in our minds, we had already traveled 21,000 miles, from Alaska and the Arctic Circle to Mexico and the Tropic of Cancer to Florida and Low Country USA. We would travel 80,000 more miles, but the pattern was set early on. Because of consistently new experiences, activities, places, sights and people, boredom never had the chance to set in. And the ability to go boondocking or dry camping— without being connected to water, electric, or sewer hook-up—brought us closer to nature and the outdoors.

This chapter may give you an idea of some of the benefits and disadvantages of RVing that are applicable to shorter RV trips like escaping on weekends and even with seasonal vacations. But if you are considering fulltime RVing or making the RV your home, this may help you reach a more informed decision.

BENEFITS OF FULLTIME RVING
We enjoyed the following benefits of fulltime RVing:

1. Consistently experiencing new things-to-do
2. Consistently seeing new places and sights
3. Consistently meeting new people

4. Being close to nature and the outdoors
5. Getting a larger and continually refreshing view of life
6. Enjoying the positive kind of stress

While we were still getting used to each other as a couple, RVing gave us a chance to develop a more accepting view of life. We adapted more easily to differences in daily living among countries, regions, states, cities, and towns. With a more laid back life, we also had time to reflect on universal themes and larger concerns.

Though there was a lot of stress looking for campgrounds, hooking and unhooking, planning itineraries, mapping sights to see and choosing activities to do, it was the positive kind of stress; it wasn't the kind where you earnestly prayed that your situation would change or wished that you were somewhere else. It was the kind that made you say, "I am so tired" with a smile on your face. And it was the kind that allowed you to sleep soundly at night after a day well spent.

DISADVANTAGES OF FULLTIME RVING
But we also experienced the following disadvantages:

1. Loss of a sense of stability
2. The risks of many unfamiliar situations
3. Stress on bonds with family and friends
4. Inconsistency in involvement with worthwhile causes
5. Loss of income
6. Inconsistent healthcare

The very benefits of having something new all the time also brought the disadvantages of instability and a preponderance of unfamiliar situations, especially in the beginning with our smaller twenty-four-foot RV. Once, in Chicken, Alaska, I ended up finishing my bath using the cold water in the sink (Brrrrr). But that is nothing compared to the feelings I sometimes got, when questions like "am I going to make it through this" and thoughts of "maybe we ought to just settle down" came up.

But more telling was the stress on bonds with family and friends, and the inability to continue the humanitarian causes we used to support. Technology has definitely helped with bonding—skype, webcam, cell phones, broadband access, laptops, the internet, Facebook, etc.—but the benefits of touch and feel were not there. And, since we had practically a new parish each or every other week, we could not participate in a regular ministry. In hindsight, we could have parked our RV near our children's homes for longer times; and maybe, in Louisiana, parked our RV and helped build homes for Katrina victims.

What younger people would find most disturbing, however, is the loss of regular income. We found out later that there are options like "work camping" (see workampingJobs.com or Work-For-RVers-and-Campers.com), parking your RV at Amazon distribution centers for seasonal jobs, or getting a portable career such as monetizing travel blogs. For retired people like us who have grown allergic to work, we just became more frugal than usual. It was not a big issue. It just meant spending within one's means which was already second nature to us, anyway.

But the disadvantage that made us settle down sooner rather than later was inconsistent healthcare. Again in hindsight, we should have established a central location where we could return regularly a couple of months a year so that a family physician, a dentist, and an ophthalmologist could take care of monitoring our health. Since we didn't, we had a few health issues that bothered us more as time went on. We had several wake-up calls before we finally decided to end our never-ending RVing honeymoon.

But today, we have come to the same conclusions as we did before, with a little difference. Adopt fulltime RVing as a cruising lifestyle only if you can include healthcare in the equation. Otherwise, just do shorter trips, return to a home base regularly, and take care of your health consistently. One thing is sure though: If you do it right, fulltime RVing will save you a lot of money (please refer to Chapter 4 on Cost Comparison in the handy booklet, *Cruising in an RV*). If you love to travel, you can succumb to the lure of the open road and love every minute of it. And during this time of coronavirus, it means you can travel without a dependence on other kinds of lodging. Your home, or the extension of your home, is with you.

2

Buying Our New Home

§

Once we made the decision to do fulltime RVing, we had to buy our new home on wheels. Buying an RV was not a new experience for us; we had bought one just eight months before. That first one was a quick decision. It was an affordable option (US$10,000) for a honeymoon of roaming around North America, just about how much we spent for the wedding reception. We decided on a small RV, an off-white 24-foot Class B motorhome, a Telstar by Firan, to save on gas and to easily maneuver and park. She had enough storage space and the bedroom and bathroom could be closed off from the living area. "Vino," an electric blue Yamaha 125 scooter, became our cute "dinghy" for exploring a locale.

Pretty soon we had added 21,000 miles to "Star" and met some people who were doing fulltime RVing. We also wanted to stay longer at places, say three weeks at a time, not just a few days. So we joined a national campground network that would allow us to do that. The decision was confirmed when my youngest daughter joined us for a tour of Mexico. It did become a little too cozy for comfort; and we wanted to continue to entertain guests.

So we started knocking on RV doors at campgrounds only six months after beginning our journey, asking the owners to give us a quick look-see of their rigs. And after our first three-week stay in Wildwood, Florida, we had a pretty good idea of what we wanted in our new home. In Orlando we chanced upon an RV show, got to inspect a 27-foot fifth wheel—a non-motorized RV that must be pulled by a pick-up truck as opposed to a travel trailer that can be pulled by other vehicles. We were surprised with a reasonable quote. My husband could not believe how affordable a bigger RV could be.

One of the campers we met at a potluck dinner referred us to Lazy Days, the largest RV dealer in the US, selling thousands of RVs a year. We were offered a complimentary stay at the Tampa, Florida location—they have added eight other US locations since then. What was supposed to be a four-night/three-day visit became an eleven-day/ten-night odyssey. When we left, Bill was "nervously" driving a 37.5-foot Class A motorhome—these motorized RVs come as campers, Class A, B, and C—towing a red Saturn for a dinghy (Saturns were the easiest to hook to an RV).

The motto on the main building says, "Lazy Days. If you love RVing, this is home." Their unique business model is based on the premise that the only really profitable relationship in the industry is a long-term one, looking at supplying all the RVs one may need in a lifetime. The buyers must be so satisfied with his initial purchase that they go back to trade-in for the next.

The 500-acre Tampa grounds were always busy with hundreds of RVs coming and going. There were 270+ service bays and an inventory of thousands of rigs. In fact, also on the lot was a branch of the nationwide RV store and service provider Camping World, the popular country dining chain Cracker Barrel, a Quality Inn hotel, and the popular Flying J travel center. A card-carrying member is treated to day-long Starbucks coffee, meals at the Café, a private site at the campground, newspapers on your steps in the morning, a heated pool and spa, tennis courts, and free seminars about everything you need to know about RVing.

Without sales people pressuring us, we were shown many models, and soon we pinpointed a few for our shortlist. My husband couldn't picture me driving a pick-up, and had high hopes that I could help with some driving if we had a small compact car as a dinghy. So, fifth-wheels were eliminated. We also planned to stay at most only three weeks at a campground, so that eliminated travel trailers. It had to be a Class A motorhome.

Based on four factors—maneuverability, layout, aesthetics, and miles per gallon—we came up with four options to evaluate more closely. To come up with the final choice, we had to consider both quality and financial cost. The financial score was a combination of the amount we had to pay for the RV and the probable cost of maintaining it over at least five years. This maintenance cost was dependent on the technical state and age of the RV. The quality score, on the other hand, was a rating on how well our needs and wants were going to be met. Our needs were a refrigerator, a stove, a microwave, an oven, a bathroom suite, bedside tables and lamps, a dinette instead of a table and chairs, a sofa bed instead of a jack-knife, a big-enough sink, ample kitchen counter space, a light neutral color/trim, more flooring instead of carpet, a queen-size bed, and two high definition TVs/DVDs with iPod connections. The wants were only two: a study desk/dresser and a washer/dryer.

The motorhome that came out on top was much longer than we'd originally wanted, so I was more nervous than my husband during the test drive. But he said we'd get used to it as others have. I dropped the dresser idea since make-up would not help that much at my age anyway. We bought the washer/dryer combo and had it installed. *Voila*, the rig was made perfect.

And then we had a new matrix of things to buy for the new home—a vase here, a painting there, and flowers everywhere. In the very week we got our new home, we entertained two couples on two separate occasions, and invited a host of others from around the world to visit and stay with us. The RV lifestyle was on. Our Newmar Mountain Aire became our new home, and a Saturn was our dinghy.

3

CAMPING AROUND AMERICA

§

Thousand Trails in which we were members had eighty-one campgrounds supplemented by the Resorts of Distinction's 125, giving us a total of 206 RV resorts to choose from. Both gave us all the campgrounds we needed at different points in time. Of course, we could also stay in the state and national parks, beachfronts, rest areas and Walmart, to supplement our choices.

This network gave us our share of glamorous neighborhoods. "Glamping," a recent trend coined from the phrase glamorous camping, technically refers to luxury cabins and tents. I like to think that it all started with RVing. Even with such great neighborhoods, however, fulltime RVing allows you to get up and go when you find out you do not like your neighbors. That was not frequently the reason we left. We were simply on a mission to discover all of North America.

In fact, we lived in more than a hundred homes in the first five years of RVing; our home was wherever the RV happened to be parked. Technically speaking, however, the RV is our only home so the statement should read "more than a hundred neighborhoods." In this piece, I list our picks for the best neighborhoods we have ever lived in. I also name each campground as one of the four types from my own method of classifying them by location and amenities (as described in Chapter 2 of the handy booklet, *Cruising in an RV*).

KIRK KREEK CAMPGROUND ON BIG SUR

We were looking for a place to stop for the night as we negotiated the drive along Highway 1 running through Big Sur. As we left Monterrey Bay, Carmel, and Pebble Beach, one stunning scene after another became the fine, slow-motion movie we were privileged to watch.

We had made no reservations, so it was incredible that we found a National Forest Service site right there between the Sta. Lucia Mountains and the deep blue Pacific Ocean. It was the perfect place, a great *nature park*. We could hike to the small beach below through some trails along the ridge. Although the beaches of Big Sur are unsuitable for swimming because of unpredictable currents and frigid temperatures, we loved the unique view of the ocean. A photo of Bill on a chair carved out of a tree perched on a ridge has become, for me, a priceless treasure.

At the campground, I met my very first author— and I would meet a lot more during our RVing odyssey—who, by a sizzling campfire, told me stories about how he got started, how he finally got a book published, and how he painstakingly sold every copy. Other neighbors included young campers who ran out of water to whom generous Bill gave half of ours. It was a neighborhood I would not forget, even if we just stayed for two days and a night.

YOSEMITE/SEQUOIA NATIONAL PARKS IN CENTRAL CALIFORNIA

At Sequoia, in what is called the Giant Forest, five of the ten largest trees in the world stand. The General Sherman, largest living thing in the world, is 275 feet tall with over 50,000 cubic feet of mass and a base diameter of thirty-six and a half feet. This puny Filipina never dreamed she would witness such an awesome creation. That there were little bears walking around made me feel more awed than scared. We just kept a healthy distance.

But nearby Yosemite is the park many consider to be the most beautiful of all national parks. There are three main sections. The fields, clear streams, and waterfalls in Yosemite Valley were ablaze with the colors of fall. Up at Tuolumne Meadows, we still found lots of snow as we stood there overlooking the tops of the mountains. At Glacier Point, higher than the mountains, is a spectacular vista of gargantuan gray granite rocks, including the famous Half Dome.

The national park has several campgrounds, all *nature resorts*, and we stayed at the only one with available slots—again we had no reservations—nearest the entrance, farthest from the amenities and facilities. Yosemite had become a small city with a department and grocery store, specialty retail shops, movie theaters, restaurants and fast food outlets.

At our campground we grilled hotdogs and marshmallows with a group of new college graduates, who were taking a break before they started to work. During our raucous nights with them, I decided to start writing a blog and to title it *Generation Z. Cruising in an RV. It's Not about Age. It's about Lifestyle*. Those two nights made me describe a Generation Z not defined by a range of years, but by a common love for the outdoors and RVing, like what those boys and us felt so strongly as a common bond.

Grand Tetons/Yellowstone National Parks in Montana/Wyoming

Without any reservations—the system is first-come, first-served— we arrived early at the Grand Teton National Park and got five nights. Grand Teton is a breath-taking experience. There are three well-known peaks that stand close together: the Grand Teton, the highest at 13,770 ft., the Middle Teton, and the South Teton. Mt. Teewinot is another peak that is the most pointed and closest to Grand, while Mt. Moran, a little further removed, features a famous skillet glacier. The fifty-mile mountain range sprung up when the

Teton fault moved and sank the valley below. There are no foothills, making the peaks even more jaggedly dramatic.

From there we also got four nights at nearby Yellowstone National Park. There are about 900 geysers in the world; over 500 of them are in Yellowstone. The park is home not just to geysers—like the tallest in the world at 400 feet, Steamboat, or Old Faithful that gushes faithfully every ninety minutes to as high as 150 feet—but also mud pots (Mud Volcano), steam vents (Black Growler), and hot springs (Grand Prismatic Spring). There are lodges, inns, cabins, RV campgrounds, and tent villages from which to base an exploration of Yellowstone. Seven areas are equipped with general stores, service stations, dining facilities, and other amenities.

It wasn't all that neighborly in the two campgrounds, however; everybody was busy scouring a vast acreage filled with wonders. That's where we saw herds of bison that clogged the roadways and walked alongside us. We were so close to nature and its bounties but also so well equipped with everything that we needed, just like at home. They were grand *nature resorts*.

Big Pine Key in the Florida Keys

As we drove through the Florida Keys from Miami, the long narrow Overseas Highway had blue-green water and swaying palms on both sides. For us, it ranked alongside the Dempster Highway going up the Arctic Circle in Canada and Highway 1 in Big Sur along the West Coast for scenic beauty. We stayed at the Sunshine Key Resort that sits on a piece of sandy land jutting out into the sea with water on all three sides. The campground covered almost the entire Key.

We had such a fun-loving crowd for neighbors. Everyone was sunbathing around the huge pool. Country music was continuously provided by a live entertainer while tropical drinks were served for free throughout the afternoons. There was even an exercise room, a good country store, and a marina filled with boats. And Key West was only a bus ride away. We thought that if we were to settle down, this kind of resort living is what we would like to have. This was another great *nature resort*.

VIEWPOINT RV AND GOLF RESORT IN ARIZONA

This is the least nature-inspired of our favorite neighborhoods; it is a *city resort*. Viewpoint is the place we chose for our six-month fall/winter hibernation for the last three years of our fulltime RVing. It has three clubhouses, two golf courses, ten tennis courts, a ball park, ten pickleball courts, two fitness centers, ten craft rooms, a computer room, a library, fifty organized clubs, and a bar/grille. And it's right in the middle of the Phoenix SMSA of six million people. The owners of the RVs beside us included us in their parties, their games, and their fire pit talks at night. They have become our lifelong friends. We have even visited them in their primary homes. Some of them have settled fulltime in Viewpoint, like us. They were the foremost reason we settled in Viewpoint.

The last type of campground, a *city park,* is what we chose whenever we wanted to be near the home of a child or a friend or a city we wanted to explore. They typically are places to return to for sleep. We have so many more favorite neighborhoods but for these five alone, it would be worth your getting an RV from any reputable dealer, either to be owned or rented. We hope you choose a great neighborhood though. Be careful or you might get hooked.

4

An Epic Alaska Road
Trip in Our Own RV

Note: This was an article I wrote for and published by TravelAwaits.

W e drove Star, our own RV, up through the 1,390-mile long
Alaska Highway from Dawson Creek, British Columbia to
Delta Junction, Alaska. It was not only for the adventure on the
scarcely traveled highway built for logistics needs in WWII; it was
also because we wanted to have an RV to freely explore the nation's
last frontier when we got there.

After a week of traveling through really small towns and over per-
mafrost-ridden roads, we quickly called it a night when we reached
our first Alaska campground, the RV Village in Tok. The next morning, however, we woke up to a thick haze from forest fires raging
from Anchorage to Fairbanks. We postponed going to Anchorage to
visit Bill's daughter, and instead went southeast to the fishing town
of Valdez, about four and a half hours away, to allow time for the
smog to lift. Such is the freedom of movement an RV can give you.

VALDEZ, ALASKA

On the way to Valdez in southeastern Alaska, there were showers and, as we lost cell signals, the glaciers seemed to be just tiny patches of white. As Star negotiated a bend on Richardson Highway, however, forty minutes before reaching Valdez, a huge white mountain suddenly appeared. It was Worthington Glacier. The State Recreational Site had ample grounds, and after parking, Bill easily climbed the glacier and brought back a piece of frozen blue ice to keep in Star's freezer.

Valdez, the Alaska town nearest the disastrous 1989 Exxon oil tanker spill, has recovered and now has a population of 4,000. We settled at a nature campground called Allison Park. At the marina, low-lying clouds encircled the boats and fishermen lined the banks; the waters were thick with pink salmon. A road sign led us up into the hills where we came across a section of the Alaska gas pipeline and berry bushes that the bears had ravaged. I thought, better the berries than us!

ANCHORAGE, ALASKA

After the second day, we drove to Anchorage, five hours away, and parked Star at the driveway in the home of Bill's daughter. With a population of almost 300,000, downtown Anchorage was fun, with many replicas of bears, the sod log cabin Visitor Center, and the many reminders of the legendary Iditarod race around town. We looked for Alaskan souvenirs, including ivory and fur products. And of course, we had to try Moose's Tooth Pub and Pizzeria, for the best pizza in town. But we wanted to explore more of the last frontier and so did Cristine.

HOMER, ALASKA

All three of us took the RV to Homer, the halibut fishing capital of the world, at the southwestern tip of the Kenai Peninsula. It has a famous spit jutting out into the cold blue waters of Kachenak Bay. Father and daughter fished to their hearts' content so we had a fish feast that night. The next day we went hunting for souvenirs at the quaint shops in the colorful huts perched above the waters along the spit shore. A great seafood dinner at the famous Salty Dawg Café capped our visit, and we posted a 100 Philippine peso and US $1 bills on its currency-covered ceilings and walls.

WHITTIER, ALASKA

The next weekend, we went to Whittier, Alaska, a small town of about 200 (double in summer) on the western edge of south central Alaska. Cruise lines use it as a departure port for their Gulf of Alaska

Cruises. It is only sixty-two road miles southeast of Anchorage, separated from Alaska's road system by a 2.5-mile-long tunnel shared by one-way alternating auto and railroad traffic, itself an adventure to go through.

The Phillips Cruise took us to see twenty-six glaciers up close, some rising to 1,700 feet above sea level. A high speed catamaran, with huge windows in two enclosed decks and extensive outside viewing areas, took us to Resurrection Bay and the College Fjords. We saw sea otters, seals, porpoises, sea lions and whales, but it was Surprise Glacier, a blue tidewater glacier which had contributed pieces of ice floating on the waters around the vessel, that surprised us. It was just like a scene from *Titanic*. The crew even served us glacial blue margaritas with ice harvested from the waters.

DENALI NATIONAL PARK

It was sad, since we knew another visit to Alaska would not happen soon, but we had to say goodbye to Cristine, eager to explore Denali National Park, just five hours north. It was established in 1917 as the first national park to conserve wildlife. At six million acres—larger than the State of Massachusetts—the park is home to several RV campgrounds. North America's highest peak, the awe-inspiring, 20,320 foot Mount McKinley, is the park's most prominent feature.

The only way to get to the heart of Denali was to backpack or ride the shuttle buses. We chose the bus that would take us to Eielson, the nearest point to Mt. McKinley. Our driver was great at looking for wildlife for us. He pointed to a grizzly bear walking on the road in front of us, a Dall sheep grazing on a mountain side, a wolf nestled among the grass, and caribou resting down in the valley.

But when we reached Eielson, the heavy fog hiding Mt. McKinley had not lifted at all. We could not buy any of the merchandise with the words, "I am part of the 30% that saw Mt. McKinley." The forecast was that it would not clear for the next few days, so we spent our last day learning a lot at the Murie Science Learning Center and visiting with hardy Huskies at the Iditarod sled dog training facility.

FAIRBANKS, ALASKA

Fairbanks, only two hours north from Denali, is the second largest city in the state with over 35,000 in population. We spent a lot of time at the University of Alaska, Fairbanks where from a viewpoint we finally got a glimpse of Mt. McKinley, albeit 100 miles away. I found artichoke plants at the university's nursery and musk oxen at its Large Animals Research Station. We also spent time at The Museum of the North, a gallery of Alaskan history and animals, including exhibits of unique prehistoric Alaskan dinosaurs.

In downtown Fairbanks, after visiting some craft shops, we discovered colorful artsy building air vents on street corners, and invested one afternoon hunting all twelve of them. But when we stopped by the Fairbanks Visitors Center to ask about how we could see the Northern Lights and get to the Arctic Circle, we were told the conditions were not good. That was as huge a disappointment as not seeing Mt. McKinley.

NORTH POLE, ALASKA

So we moved on to North Pole, Alaska, just thirty minutes north of Fairbanks with a population of about 2,000. It isn't the true geographic North Pole but it was more fun! Streets were named Santa Claus Lane, Snowman Road, Kris Kringle Drive, etc. Almost everything was in a candy cane motif. The Visitor Information Center was an authentic rustic Alaskan log cabin where both of its "Welcome to the North Pole" signs were very Christmassy. We also visited The Pole of North Pole, one of two poles created to symbolize the special place on earth. The other one was pushed out of a plane over the actual location which is still 1,700 miles north.

We stayed at the Santa Land RV Park. Its entrance had life-sized reindeer and a 200-foot Santa. Beside the park was the town's famous Santa Claus House, full of Christmas goodies. From there, you can send Christmas cards to all your loved ones postmarked North Pole, Alaska, like we did. And you can have your photo taken on Santa's lap inside the House; but not the world's largest fiberglass Santa outside, 42-feet tall, weighing almost a thousand pounds.

CHICKEN, ALASKA

Our next destination was Seattle, Washington, not Canada, so we followed another route going back, more directly south than the Alaska Highway. The first stop was Chicken, Alaska, a town of thirty-two during summer—seven at wintertime. The road was all gravel. There were two campgrounds, one with gold-panning activities and the other with a country store. We stayed at the former, up the hill, where we were rewarded with a spectacular sunset later.

The following day we drove along the Top of the World Highway that leads to Canada. There were endless mountaintops carpeted by the reddish-gold alpine tundra of early fall. The US-Canada border was unlike any other border town. There was no one around except for my husband, me, and the immigration officer. Then, together with Star and Vino, our RV and scooter tandem, we rode the ferry to Dawson City, Yukon's capital during the Gold Rush.

HYDER, ALASKA

From the Yukon, we dropped south down to British Columbia, where we took a right to the Stewart-Cassiar Highway, also known as Glacier Highway, toward the town of Stewart, population 500, for its reported great fishing. We missed the season by a day, however, and there were no more fishing boats for hire. But we found out that a town of about 100, Hyder, was just two miles down the road.

It is the southernmost point of Alaska and home to the Salmon Glacier, the fifth largest glacier in North America. As we went fifteen miles of muddy dirt/gravel road up the hill, it slowly made its appearance. The pictures we took at the summit did not give it justice. And we paid a high price to see the spectacle. I can only imagine the brutal punishment it was for Star.

Then, back at the foot of the hill, we found a good-sized black bear hunting for all the salmon he could find on Fish Creek. At times he was a mere twenty feet from us but we must have been incognito. When his show was over, it was already getting dark, so Bill decided to park our RV by the roadside for the night. I could not sleep well until he assured me that the bear was too full to look for me. It was a fitting finale for a perfect summer month exploring the Alaska mystique. We were glad we brought our RV; it gave us the freedom to explore the last frontier.

5

FINDING CHRISTMAS
ON TREASURE ISLAND

C hristmas 2011, just two years after we started RVing, felt different from the other Christmases Bill and I had spent together. In 2007, it was white and freezing at -31 degrees C in Calgary, Alberta. We were just in courtship mode, but I wanted to spend the holidays with my second daughter and her family. In 2008, after our wedding, we were with my eldest daughter and family, wet and cold in Seattle, Washington. In 2009 on our first Christmas Eve in the RV, it turned sunny and warm at the Suwannee River Music Park in Florida. Christmas 2010 was again in Seattle because I was waiting for my US CIS interview. But in 2011, as soon as we had arrived at the Thousand Trails Resort in Orlando, Florida, it became particularly hard to find the spirit.

The morning after we checked in, right after breakfast, Bill felt severe sharp pains in his chest; then both arms started to get numb and heavy. Soon after, he felt lightheaded and dizzy. He still had the presence of mind to use our blood pressure monitor. It read 166/98 (way above his usual 110/70). That was when we got scared, quickly got into the car, and hurriedly drove to the nearest Urgent Care facility, only a mile from the campground.

But we were immediately turned away: the doctor said we had better hurry to the nearest hospital, the Heart of Florida, twelve miles away. We were lucky we were in a city resort in Orlando and not some far away nature park. Knowing that I was nervous, with few driving skills and unfamiliar with American roads, Bill who was still in pain drove us to the hospital. He truly felt that would be less stressful than watching me try to drive and even possibly getting us into an accident.

He was supposed to be the healthier of us two. I was the one who was having all sorts of issues. He was always reminding me about our promise to give each other at least thirty years even if we had found each other at this late age. We had just celebrated four years of being together; just started our cruising lifestyle two and a half years before. And we had such a *looooong* bucket list to complete. In fact, we'd only just begun.

The ER staff jumped on his case right away. By about 1 pm, the cardiologist on call told me that Bill had had a heart attack, quickly transferred him to the ICU, and ordered a heart catheterization for the following morning. My heart sank. That was an invasive procedure. Even if death was rare, there could be complications. All sorts of images raced through my mind. But Bill wanted to have it done, because not doing anything could be deadly, if not more. Besides, they did about 200 such procedures in the Heart of Florida every month. It is, in fact, considered routine. But I was just simply too scared.

I could not stay overnight with him in the ICU and I had to go back to the campground by nyself. I ended up driving the car onto a sidewalk, almost right onto a concrete fence. That's when the tears fell unabashedly. But I got out of there, made it to the campground, very slowly.

That first night alone in the RV was tough. As soon as I got in, I fixed myself a small bowl of hot soup. Then I reached out to family and friends. I called each of my children, Bill's sister, and friends we had just met in the previous RV park. Their voices calmed my truly frayed nerves. I managed to get four hours of sleep. Unfortunately and understandably, Bill had tossed and turned more in his hospital bed.

The waiting room outside the catheterization lab was not a good place to be that morning. The courtesy TV was on a program that was discussing the stresses of a funeral with some grieving folks. But the procedure was over at noon and the doctor called me in. Bill had two blockages, one 100%, the other 75%. The cardiologist had inserted two stents to open the more damaged artery. He said it would have been too much for Bill to bear the procedure on the other one at the same time. So it was scheduled for mid-January to give his heart some time to rest.

The before and after pictures of the catheterization showed the amazing opening of new blood pathways already feeding his weakened heart muscles. I was so glad he had it done. And I became an "experienced" driver in the process, after three days. Bill is a lucky guy, and not only because he is married to me.

We both thanked the Lord for giving us a manageable wake-up call and making it a quick recovery. Possible risk factors could not have been about bad diet or not exercising regularly. Bill attributed it to genetics—his mother and grandmother both had cardiovascular diseases— and age which he finally had to admit, factors he could not do anything about except for the matter of about fifteen extra pounds he was then determined to lose.

So we went to find the Christmas spirit away from our everyday home. We felt we needed a vacation from the RV. We booked a time-share unit at the Sand Pebble Resort in Treasure Island, Florida. It is one of thirteen beaches around the Tampa Bay area, the region of west central Florida adjacent to Tampa Bay, almost two hours from Orlando. It is also known as the Tampa-St. Petersburg-Clearwater Metropolitan Statistical Area, with an estimated population of four million.

We had almost forgotten how comfortable condo living could be. Our one-bedroom unit was spacious enough for two couples and had a view of the Gulf of Mexico from the balcony. At the ground floor of the resort, there was a hot tub, a heated pool, pool tables, and a bar. Every afternoon there was an activity, be it bingo, ice cream socials, count the shells, etc. But it was the quiet beach at the back that was the best of all for tranquil rest and meditation.

Like in previous years, we got busy looking for stocking stuffers for our Christmas Eve opening of gifts. Bill and I happily lost each other at the Mustang Florida Flea Market for an hour to hunt for the little treasures. Not satisfied with our haul, we went to the Tyrone Square Mall to complete our search. Each stash was carefully guarded and hidden so no intruder could take a peek until the proper time. I spent a total of $25; I bet Bill spent so much more.

The following day we went for a long drive along Gulf Boulevard connecting all ten barrier islands and thirteen beaches, collectively known as the Tampa Bay Beaches. It was never-ending miles of beach homes, condo-resorts, and palm trees. The best of them all was to the north in Clearwater, Florida, just before reaching the Honeymoon Island State Park. It was aptly called Clearwater Beach, famous for white powdery sand, just like the Philippines's best beaches. We discovered a beach haven much bigger than the Keys, adjacent to a busy metropolitan area; another place where we could conceivably settle.

The next day we discovered legendary Ybor City in Greater Tampa, Florida, the former "Cigar Capital of the World" after Don Vincente Martinez-Ybor moved his cigar factory from Key West to Tampa in the early 1900s. Other cigar-makers followed, building their own factories. Immigrants from Spain, Cuba and Sicily came to work in them, and Romanian merchants opened stores while German lithographers brought the latest in technology to print the cigar labels. Today, it is an entertainment and arts district, with lively demonstrations of hand-rolling cigars.

On Christmas Eve, Bill and I heard a joyous mass at St. John Vianney in St. Pete's Beach, Florida with a little pageant of kids as angels, shepherds, and the Three Kings around the Nativity Scene at the altar. Then we came home to our *Noche Buena* of maple/honey glazed ham, Dubliner cheese, fancy crackers, and Christmas *stollen*. At almost the stroke of midnight, Bill got his new polar bear jammies, pristine white hankies, and a heart warmer for cold hands. Yes, he definitely spent more; men's love language has traditionally been gifts. I got new diamond earrings to replace the ones I had lost, new fit-over dark glasses to replace the pair I had lost, and a purse so that I don't lose any more things. Talks with my children on the phone capped our Christmas Eve.

After a light breakfast of left-overs, off we went to complete our drive to the south end of Gulf Boulevard for a couple more beaches and the feat of engineering called the Sunshine Skyway Bridge. Back at the condo, a light lunch preceded our one last trip to the hot tub and Skype sessions with Bill's children. And to cap a relaxing vacation, we went to see *Mission Impossible* on the big screen and dined at Joey's Famous Pizza Kitchen in downtown St. Petersburg, Florida to spare me from more cooking—or Bill from **my** cooking.

Christmas 2011 was surely different. We found the spirit in bits and pieces everywhere, as we recreated Christmas traditions in a brand new place. It was good we decided to return briefly to life in a condo. But we found it most in in Him. The Christmas spirit, after all, is the special kinship He has made possible for all of us to share, and we were reminded why we met and why He put us together. After all, we are a couple who may have found each other late in life but oh, so early in our dreams.

6

TURNING WOUNDS
INTO WISDOM

§

We used our RV to visit each of the forty-nine states in mainland America. Many were memorable, but none inspired
me more than our visit to Georgia. As I am writing this, the state is
experiencing a resurgence of coronavirus cases. It has also been a hot
spot for the protests against the remaining sentiments of systemic
racism. As a matter of fact, it has become front and center during
the 2020 post-election investigations. But I know that Georgia will
rise from these difficulties again.

In 2012, as I was visiting the state, I was reminded of what Oprah
once said: "turn wounds into wisdom." And that is what we saw in
the state, judging by the many great institutions it has fostered out
of the ravages of war, years of division, and adversity for its people
since the Civil War years. And they are the institutions that are at
center stage right now, with the pandemic and the protests. It was

a truly different kind of sight-seeing when we explored its capital Atlanta and a smaller city to the south, Americus. I hope you get to carve out such special itineraries to the same spiritually uplifting places.

THE CENTER FOR DISEASE CONTROL

The world will forever be grateful for this great institution. It was created in 1946 as a US federal agency under the Department of Health and Human Services. Headquartered in Druid Hills in Greater Atlanta, the Center for Disease Control works to protect public health and safety. And I am so glad I was able to see first-hand how it conducts its work.

The center had a desk that took care of visitors like us and maintained many exhibits that explained the different parts of what they do. Bill even donned the well-known safe suit worn by epidemiologists who have to risk their lives and go into infected and infectious places. We learned about the major successes the CDC has had in averting world health crises, making the world a safer place.

In 1955 it traced contaminated poliomyelitis vaccine to a California lab. Two years later, it tracked the massive influenza epidemic, positioning the agency's future as a leader in disease surveillance. In 1977 CDC also played a key role in one of the greatest triumphs of public health, the eradication of smallpox through an "eradication escalation" technique. A little later on, it found the cause(s) of Legionnaires disease and toxic-shock syndrome. And in 1981, CDC successfully identified the fatal disease subsequently named acquired immunodeficiency syndrome (AIDS) and then led in the efforts to control it. Today it is again at front and center in the fight against the novel coronavirus.

MARTIN LUTHER KING, JR. NATIONAL HISTORIC SITE

Martin Luther King, Jr. (1929–1968) is an iconic figure in the advancement of civil rights in the US and around the world, using nonviolent methods following the teachings of Mahatma Gandhi. A Baptist minister, King led the 1955 Montgomery Bus Boycott sparked by Rosa Parks. Then he helped found the Southern Christian Leadership Conference in 1957 and served as its first president. King's efforts led to the 1963 March on Washington, where he delivered his "I Have a Dream" speech, leading to the historic passage of the Civil Rights Act in 1964.

Because of his work, he became the youngest person to receive the Nobel Peace Prize until 2014. In 1965, the historic Selma march led to the historic passage of the Voting Rights Act in the same year.

By the time of his death in 1968, he had refocused his efforts on ending poverty and stopping the Vietnam War. Sadly, he was assassinated on April 4, 1968, in Memphis, Tennessee. It is no wonder that the Martin Luther King, Jr. Day was established as a U.S. federal holiday in 1986. No other American is so honored, not even Washington or Lincoln.

We were fortunate to have visited The MLKJ National Historic Site in Atlanta, Georgia. It includes the museum, the adjacent Baptist church from which he preached, his home just a block away, and his tomb with an inspiring eternal flame. How I wish he were here today to lead the Black Lives Matter movement that exploded after the unjust death of George Floyd at the hands of police in Minneapolis. Perhaps he could give another monumental speech that would calm the waters and lead to the ultimate eradication of any remaining racism. This time he could entitle it: "I Have a Wish," to echo our joint hope that all of us live peacefully as loving brethren in this great land.

THE COCA-COLA COMPANY

The Coca-Cola Company is perhaps the greatest beverage corporation in the world. Its flagship product Coke was invented in 1886 by pharmacist John Stith Pemberton in Columbus, Georgia. The formula and brand were bought by Asa Candler, who incorporated The Coca-Cola Company in 1892. It now offers more than 500 brands in nearly 200 countries and sells over 1.6 billion servings a day. It is the world's best known brand. It is a story that should inspire businesses, big and small, worldwide. I know that—as former Managing Director of SAP Philippines—the huge enterprise has successfully leveraged on SAP software to drive its business.

Headquartered in Atlanta, it operates a great tourist destination in the city, the World of Coca Cola. It is a complete museum with a 4D Theater featuring "The Secret Ingredient"; a Taste-It Room where you can sample sixty-four different coke flavors plus concoct your own; and a Red Room with memorabilia of the company and the product over the years. You can even have your picture taken with the Coke Polar Bear, buy great Coke-branded items from a Room of Souvenirs, and join a tour of the manufacturing/bottling process.

CNN

When I spent many a night in various hotels as part of my globe-trotting career in computers, the TV news channel was my constant companion. I felt some excitement as I saw the familiar letters on the façade of its Atlanta center. And I was even more excited to learn it offered studio tours. I got to see how the news room oper-ated behind the busy scenes.

CNN was founded in 1980 by Ted Turner. It became the first to provide 24-hour television news coverage and the first all-news television channel in the US. As of 2010, CNN was available in over 100 million U.S. households, 890,000 American hotel rooms, and 195 countries. The proliferation of news channels over the years that followed CNN is testament to the great idea it was and the good service it has provided.

With the coronavirus pandemic, the protest movement, and the November elections very much in the airwaves, I have had to tune in a lot to CNN lately. But sadly I also have to spend a lot of time with Fox News; otherwise, I will not get a well-rounded view. I just wish CNN would seize the leadership again and become a neu-tral force moderating the highly polarized and explosive climate we are all in right now.

Habitat for Humanity/Jimmy Carter

Habitat for Humanity is an international NGO with its international headquarters located in Americus, Georgia and its administrative headquarters in Atlanta. The organization has 1,500 US satellite offices and five area offices located around the world. Its mission is to "eliminate poverty housing and homelessness from the world and to make decent shelter a matter of conscience and action." As a Christian housing ministry, it builds homes using volunteer labor that are sold at no profit and with highly affordable monthly payments.

I was very inspired to see first-hand where Habitat started and to visit the nearby birthplace and boyhood home of Jimmy Carter. At 95, Carter is the longest living American president, and still goes on a Carter-Habitat project each year with a thousand or so volunteers. It was personal for me. I was general manager of MegaLink—the ATM consortium of banks in the Philippines that interconnected the ATMs all over the country through a com-puter-operated switch—when my staff and I built a home for the Philippine Chapter of Habitat. A Philippine nonprofit called Gawad Kalinga has become popular extending the Habitat vision to provide not just at-cost homes but also funds and trains for the establish-ment of livelihoods.

We even found two bonuses in Atlanta. The first was the Flat Iron Building, the city's second skyscraper. It was completed in 1897 on a wedge-shaped block, five years before New York's own version, placing it on the National Register of Historic Places. Second, Atlanta is host to the home of Margaret Mitchell. She won the Pulitzer Prize in 1937 for *Gone with the Wind*, one of the most popular books of all time, having sold more than thirty million cop-ies. The film adaptation of the book, released in 1939, became the highest-grossing film in the history of Hollywood, getting a record-breaking ten Academy Awards. But current protest movements are trying to highlight all reminders of the injustices African-Americans have suffered in this country. And *Gone with the Wind* is, allegedly, one of them.

This was one of the best-loved among all my blog posts. In fact, it continues to generate views every day. With today's current events, the institutions it has fostered are as relevant now as when they were founded. It will probably be a long, long time before I forget this trip to Georgia, a state that continues to "turn wounds into wisdom."

7

OPERATIONALIZING
FULLTIME RVING

§

B ill thought the title of this post strange so I looked up the word "operationalize" in the dictionary. Of the two meanings, I intended the second one, "to put into operation, start working," for this post. Fulltime RVing is a combination of relaxing while exploring. It is what you get when you use your RV as your home. It is different from how we started RVing, running around while staying at a campground for only a few days at a time.

ADVANCE, NORTH CAROLINA

Even if we had bought our new home in Florida, because of guests and parties, it was not until we got to North Carolina that we were finally able to realize the benefits of fulltime RVing. We were in Advance, an unincorporated community of 62.3 square miles on the western bank of the Yadkin River, nestled within the Piedmont Triad of Winston-Salem, High Point, and Greensboro. The country cottages along the roads were pretty with azaleas in full bloom. I even saw a mushroom farm; it consisted of piles of oak wood at Sandy Creek Farm.

In this little community, we found Forest Lake RV Resort, frequented by many locals in the area as a weekend vacation spot. Bill took out a fishing license and alternated between the small stocked lake on the property and the Yadkin River a few hundred feet away. For almost three weeks, we just kind of "chilled out," playing mini-golf and billiards, hiking the trails, and sharing dinners with fellow campers. I even beat Bill once at mini-golf and billiards. And, while he was drowning worms, my blog got a great deal of attention.

We wished the spa had been open. The peak season was Memorial Day to Labor Day, and that was when all the amenities, including two pools, were open. I had gained a few more pounds and begun to develop love handles—the negative side effect of an extended happy state—between my waist and hips. So we took to playing table tennis—I beat Bill here, too (once)—and tried playing pickleball. We also took up exercising again, including some yoga and Pilates. Alas, I realized the problem would not go away fast. Bill reminded me that I had to do something about the thing called eating, too.

Some days we ventured out of the campground and hunted for treasures around the consignment shops and flea markets in downtown Lexington, eight miles away, and Mocksville, ten miles away. I wanted to send my grandson a dinosaur/robot, and to find an ornament tree for Christmas. Instead we found a beautiful wooden five-bottle wine rack for our counter for only $18. On many days, however, we simply went to the library for faster Internet surfing.

One Sunday we went to Winston-Salem, drove around the city, and spotted a seven-foot coffee pot downtown on the façade of a local coffee shop. We also went to three vineyards to sample North Carolina wine, rumored to be making a comeback. At the end of the day, Bill treated me to my first Cracker Barrel dinner. It was quite an experience. And when we went to hear mass at the Catholic Church, we found a 1962 Corvette with the plate, "Carol's 62," and two Knights of Columbus elders in attendance. That was a special treat for me. I had been looking for a great application of my name in both North and South Carolina; "Carol's 62" on a Corvette beats Carolina Leasing or Carolina Insurance.

SALISBURY, NORTH CAROLINA

After Forest Lake, we transferred to the Bass Lake Resort, just thirty minutes away, for another three weeks in Salisbury, North Carolina. Having relaxed in Advance, we intended to run around and explore the surrounding areas more from Bass. We were not expecting it, but we were so happy we made several new friends in the campground. There were three other couples and a bachelor who all took turns making dinner for everyone to share. One of the wives was a Filipina, the first Asian I had ever encountered in the RV world.

Salisbury was a very good place to be. The city did a good job of promoting itself. Every Friday, from 5-9 PM, there was a Spring Night Out. Shops and restaurants each did something unique for the townspeople and tourists: face painting for kids, roses for moms, apple pie bites for everyone, water, candy, and balloons for all, and dancing in the streets with a live band.

We found a wine cellar in the basement of an old building. Bill had a great time there but what thrilled me was something else. Before I reached the basement, I got lost in a whole ground floor of antiques and collectibles consignment booths. And there, tucked in among old quaint stuff, was my treasure. I found the ornament tree I had been looking for. It was golden, three feet tall, and with hooks for thirty-two ornaments, for only $11. It would make a perfect little Christmas tree for our RV.

But I had another treasure to find. In fact, from the distinguished shelves of a Goodwill store, we found a Wowee RoboReptile dinosaur that was due for auction the following Tuesday. My dashing knight won for his queen the prize; I became the happiest grandma in the whole wide world, acquiring a two-foot movable dinosaur toy for my grandson for only $10.

Besides finding my treasures, I also found many great opportunities for photos of people selling their crafts. You see, I wanted to join the "I am an Entrepreneur" Photography Competition of Seven Fund. I took pictures of a face painter, a potter, and street dancers. But it was in the Webb Flea Market where I found many more: a cedar wood artist, an ax handle craftsmen, a fragrant oils retailer, a plant lady, an "elephant ear" cook, and a motorcycle airbrush specialist.

Every second Saturday Salisbury also had a Studio Crawl, a walking tour of art galleries and artists' studios. We went to the studios of the painter Robert Crum, glass fusion artist Syed Ayamm, and other art galleries. The city had a big, thriving art community, an overflow from Charlotte where the cost of living was higher. No coincidence that the town's streets had about two dozen pieces of fine public art.

Another small town, Spencer, North Carolina, was just next to Salisbury. That was where the state's famous Transportation Museum was located. Spencer was a thriving railroad depot in the early 1900s until diesel replaced the steam engines, the depot died, and the town declined, not being able to retrofit their shops fast enough. But there we saw the relics of the steam engine era, including the luxury train named Doris, of the Duke family fame.

We were surprised to discover that Charlotte, North Carolina was the second largest financial center in the US, second only to New York City. It is home to almost 700,000 people, the largest city in the state. On May 11, the day before we visited, the city had just opened the NASCAR Hall of Fame. In the Fourth Ward, at the end of the free trolley rides, is the site of historic restored Victorian-era homes and establishments. Charlotte was also the home of the National Whitewater Center, an Olympics training site. But it was the lovely Billy Graham Library that enthralled us. When the great minister died, the televised recounting of the minister's life recreated for me the fine time we had spent in that peaceful pretty place.

On the way to the Sea Grove community of potters in Star, North Carolina, we chanced upon a large group of colorful tents. I thought it was a flea market, but it turned out to be a remote control car racing event. Some of the small hobby cars had thousands of dollars invested in them. It was very interesting to meet so many so engrossed in this sport. Bill told me that the South, having many spaces of undeveloped land, is fonder of auto racing as a sport than the north.

And, finally, Sea Grove is an unbelievable community of about a hundred potters clustered around the four roads of Star, North Carolina. There we found various techniques of glazing pottery: the crystalline way, the 15th century Chinese way, etc. Some pots cost $2,500—reputedly, one-fourth the price in Atlanta. But in the Great White Oak Gallery one red Asian-inspired pot stood out from the rest. Bill and I thought that it would fit beautifully in my daughter's Zen-inspired, red-themed home in Seattle, and we bought it.

Our six-week stay in these two resorts in North Carolina gave us a full expression of how we wanted to RV. In the midst of all the big and small towns we explored, we even found some tidbits of history. Andrew Jackson had studied law there. Daniel Boone's family had trekked there. Many union soldiers had been buried near the Confederate Prison and National Cemetery there. These six weeks were definitely much better than our first phase of madly running around. We relaxed, hunted for treasures, met friends, and explored small and big cities. We had finally found how fulltime RVing should be.

8

ANOTHER EPIC ROAD TRIP TO ALASKA IN A RENTED RV

Note: This was an article I wrote for and published by TravelAwaits.

W e hadn't planned to be back in Alaska for at least three years. A trip there can be expensive, especially if you take the cruise from the mainland which does not even allow you freedom to roam the state once you get there. Driving our RV, as we had the previous year, allowed us to truly explore the state but, with the cost of gas at $4.50 to a gallon on some parts of the Alaska Highway, it was expensive; and honestly, it took all of a week. Besides, it was a case of "been there, done that."

Instead, we flew using a companion certificate of just $99, making the fare almost "buy one get one free," and stored our Class A motorhome at a resort in Monroe, Washington. When we arrived, we rented a small 22-foot Class C motorhome with good mpg, self-sufficient in remote areas, easy to maneuver in the cities, and perfect for Cristine's driveway. We were pleasantly surprised; she was getting married and that's why we had to be there. And, since it was almost off-season, the rates were surprisingly reasonable for the combined lodging and car.

KENAI PENINSULA

When the brand new couple went on their honeymoon, we took the RV to the Kenai Peninsula, to the mouth of the famous Kenai River, partly on the same road we we'd taken south to Homer the previous year. It was already later in the summer, and my pictures were not coming out as bright. But the saving grace in the Old Town of Kenai was the Holy Assumption Orthodox Church, built by the Russians at the turn of the 19th century when they still owned the land. We were even more delighted to find the Fred Meyer grocery chain which had, besides a parking place where we dry camped for the night, complimentary dump and potable water stations.

Instead of going back to Anchorage the next morning, we headed off to the other side of the peninsula, to the town of Seward, at the mouth of the Kenai Fjords National Park. It was another port for Alaska cruises but, since it was already off-season, the boats were all moored in the marina. But the shops were still open.

Eight and a half miles west, going out of the town, we saw a sign about an "Exit Glacier." That excited us and we followed the arrows, arriving at the foot of the huge Harding Ice Fields of 500 square miles. The glacier is so named because it has been receding slowly since the earliest recorded terminus in 1815——the recordings are marked all along the way——about two miles from the current one. And there I finally walked on a glacial ridge. But it was too cold; like being inside a freezer. I quickly turned back after the photo op and ran back to the RV.

Day Trips from Anchorage

We hadn't really explored Anchorage and the surrounding areas much the previous summer. There were plenty of hiking trails, all around the Chugach State Park, each one well under an hour from our base. There was Eagle River Valley as a good starting point, Mirror Lake that was well-stocked for fishing, Turnagain Arm which overlooks Potter Marsh, and the Thunderbird Falls Trail that leads to the falls.

Anchorage also offered interesting day trips. At the Alaska Wildlife Conservation Center, we photographed plenty of rescued bears, moose, musk oxen, bison, elk, and reindeer. It was good to explore the luxury Hotel Alyeska Resort with its popular ski runs for the winter, functional chair lifts, a lavish lobby, a large pond, an Art Gallery, and a log cabin steak house. I also had a great day photographing the unique scenes on the Hatcher Pass Scenic Drive, twenty-two miles of it all gravel; especially at its top, which rises 4,000 feet above sea level around the spectacular scenes of Independence Mine.

DENALI STATE PARK

And then the soggy weather changed, and we immediately jumped at the chance to see Mt. McKinley. The previous year we were denied the chance to see the mountain; it was hidden behind the clouds. There are several suggested viewing points on the 134-mile drive from Anchorage. We finally found ours at the McKinley View Lodge, where we had lunch, near the Denali State Park. With five campgrounds near the lodge, we chose to camp there for the night.

DAY TRIPS FROM FAIRBANKS

We also wanted to explore more of Fairbanks. After a little more than two hours, we reached this northern "capital" and proceeded to the Pioneer Park which had large pull-thru spaces for overnight RV parking. It is a forty-four-acre city park commemorating early Alaskan history with a Bear Gallery, a large carousel, a Dance Hall, a Palace Theater, and several museums, restaurants, and shops. Built for the Alaska-67 Centennial Exposition which commemo-rated the 100th year anniversary of the brilliant purchase of Alaska from Russia, it was the best way to get a history of Fairbanks and a view of the Alaskan way of life.

The next day we drove to Creamer's Field, a 2,200-acre bird sanctuary that is populated by sand hill cranes, mallards, and Canadian geese. The lovely refuge surrounds the former farm of Charles Creamer (1889-1974), who had established Creamer's Dairy. When he started to save waste grains from his barn to feed the migrating birds, the birds continued to flock to his farm. His home is now a quaint little museum beside the refuge.

But the highlight of our Fairbanks day trips was to Chena Hot Springs Resort, a little over an hour from Fairbanks. After lunch at the Chena Hot Springs Restaurant in the Main Log Cabin, we walked around the sod log cabins for massage therapy, the Main Lodge, and the main attraction, the outdoor hot spring pools. There were different ways of going around the property—airplane Adventure Cats, ATVs, motorcycles, horses, and canoes—all for rent.

Several group tours to cover the entire resort were also being offered. We joined the one to the Aurora Ice Museum, the world's largest such facility with ice sculptures, some of which were already ten years old. The husband and wife team that won the World Ice Sculpting Contest five times created the magnificent ice art. The temperature inside was kept at twenty-five degrees Fahrenheit and, yes, they provide the winter clothing to keep you warm inside.

The second tour was to explore the first low-temperature binary geothermal power plant ever built in Alaska. There was work on alternative energy projects, including production and use of waste vegetable oil for fuel. The second part of this tour was the Greenhouse, where the Resort uses state-of-the-art technology to nurture plants for their vegetable and flower requirements. If you are ever in Fairbanks, don't forget to go on a day trip to Chena Hot Springs Resort.

LAST HURRAH IN ANCHORAGE

We drove back to Anchorage to Christine's home but before we had to go for our scheduled flight back to Seattle, we were gifted a spectacular surprise. I never thought I would see the northern lights in early fall! These are the three requirements for seeing the phenomenon: 1) high enough "auroral" activity; 2) the least cloud cover; and 3) the least light pollution. The last one is why it is preferable to go to a more remote location. But we took a chance because the first two requirements would be met as forecasted by the University of Alaska Fairbanks Geophysical Institute.

We went up to the Anchorage Overlook Trail that went up to 1,300 feet high on Flattop Mountain. It offered a magnificent aerial view of the city. It was windy when we arrived at 10:30 pm, and we "froze" despite thick clothing layers. But a celestial party exploded when the typical greens and usual patches became active in the skies. They were faint, because of light pollution from the city, but good enough for me. There were even a few seconds when we were treated to striking rays and glimpses of pink.

And on out last weekend, we had the chance to walk on another glacier ninety minutes northeast of Anchorage. At twenty-seven miles long by four miles wide, Matanuska Glacier is the largest glacier accessible by car in the US. A valley glacier— solid ice that flows like a river under its weight about a foot a day—it began its retreat to its present day location about 10,000 years ago. Today, it still feeds the Matanuska River. We braved the challenging, muddy, and slippery hike onto the ice helped by cleats lent to us, after finally finding it by following directions on dirt roads from Glenn Highway.

Both visits to Alaska, one in our own RV and this second trip in a rented one, confirmed for us that it is indeed the country's last frontier. Renting an RV afforded us the same freedom as using our own the previous year. When air travel is no longer risky, we will go back another time to Alaska, rent another RV, and go to the westernmost and northernmost places. We will push more of Alaska's and our own limits one more time.

9

DISCOVERING THE SECRETS
OF THE MANHATTAN PROJECT

Note: This was an article I wrote for and published by TravelAwaits.

§

The success of the Manhattan Project put a swift end to a raging world war that had already killed more than 400,000 Americans at the time. The project produced Little Boy and Fat Man, the first and only atomic bombs ever dropped. They destroyed the Japanese cities of Hiroshima and Nagasaki, respectively, killing about 200,000 people, most of them Japanese civilians. Hopefully, something like it will never have to be resorted to again.

But its legacy lies in the way the project was run. It has become a model for large-scale, highly technical, hazardous wartime projects that have to be carried out in utmost secrecy. It was led by the US with support from the UK (which initiated the original Tube Alloys project) and Canada. At the height of its research and development activities, from 1942 to 1946, it was under the direction of Major General Leslie Groves of the U.S. Army Corps of Engineers.

Because we were RVing across North America for eight years, we had the opportunity to learn about the secrets of the Manhattan Project in a way that reading about them could have never done. In the span of three years, we saw three of the most important sites that contributed to its successful outcome: Oak Ridge, Tennessee, Hanover Reach, Washington, and Los Alamos, New Mexico. In fact, these three sites now jointly comprise the Manhattan Project National Historical Park that was created in 2015.

OAK RIDGE, TENNESSEE

My husband's high school classmate was a senior executive at Jacob's Engineering before his retirement. It is a company responsible for major parts of the decommissioning projects of the huge central production facilities of the Manhattan Project in Oak Ridge, Tennessee. In fact, the last part of the decommissioning was scheduled for July 2020. In June of 2010, he invited us to his home in Knoxville, Tennessee, only thirty minutes away from the Oak Ridge production facility.

He took the time to show us the full extent of the facilities at an overlook on a hill near the town. The total footprint at the time it was operational was forty-three hectares with a total of five million square feet in four floors. It was in this small Tennessee town that the biggest buildings in the world were ever built and where the biggest (and most significant) industrial projects in the world were run.

The Manhattan Project developed two types of atomic bombs during WWII: a relatively simple gun-type fission weapon using enriched uranium and a more complex implosion-type atomic bomb using plutonium. Three methods were employed for uranium enrichment and most of this work was performed at the

Clinton Engineer Works in Oak Ridge, Tennessee, codenamed "Site X."

Public Proclamation Number Two declared Oak Ridge a total exclusion area that no one could enter without military permission. It was generally known to be part of "frantic efforts" to make "tub-alloy tetroxide," the code name for ten to twelve percent enriched uranium-235. The population of Oak Ridge expanded well beyond the initial plans and peaked at 75,000 in May 1945.

Bill's high school classmate also toured us around the historic part of town and described for us how the whole town buzzed with activity during the time. At the end of the day, he showed us the documentary film, *The Secret City* which pulled together all the facts that we were hearing for the very first time. It described very clearly how the secret was kept. Everyone was sworn to secrecy. And everyone followed. It was the best introduction we could have had. We were just a year into our RVing and we hoped that we would see the complete picture of the Manhattan project.

HANFORD REACH, WASHINGTON

Just two months later we were in Washington, waiting for my appointment in Seattle in connection with my application for citizenship. As usual, we looked for national parks or national monuments to visit. That's when we accidentally came upon the Hanford Reach National Monument, named after Hanford Reach, the last non-tidal, free-flowing section of the Columbia River in the US.

At the northern end of the Reach are the White Bluffs, white cliffs rising out of the Reach for 400 feet. The lands are home to a wide variety of plants and animals, and the Hanford Reach provides one of the Northwest's best salmon spawning grounds. Additionally, forty-eight rare, threatened, or endangered animal species have found refuge on the monument grounds, as well as several insect species found nowhere else in the world.

The national monument was created in 2000, mostly from the former security buffer zone surrounding the Manhattan Project National Historic Site of about seven reactors built to produce plutonium for the Manhattan Project. The site was chosen because they were concerned that Oak Ridge was too close to an urban population center just in case there was a nuclear accident. In fact, they deemed it important that the location be as far as possible from Oak Ridge where the uranium was being produced. Hanford Reach was an hour from Richland, not a big city, also isolated, and near the Columbia River which was an ideal source of cooling water for the reactors. Hanford Engineer Works was built there, codenamed "Site W."

By July 1944 some 1,200 buildings had been erected and nearly 51,000 people were living in the construction camp. At its peak, the construction camp was the third most populous town in Washington. Hanford operated a fleet of over 900 buses (more than the city of Chicago). Today, the Hanford Reach Unit of the Manhattan Project National Historical Park contains the B-Reactor National Historic Landmark which was the reactor that produced the plutonium for Fat Man. Reactor C stands close beside it; interestingly, there is no Reactor A.

The national monument had been untouched by development or agriculture since 1943 because of its past nuclear activities. So, it has been considered an "involuntary park," a term coined by science fiction author Bruce Sterling to describe areas that, because of environmental, economic, or political reasons have been allowed to return to an overgrown, feral state. Other famous examples are Chernobyl and the Korean Demilitarized Zone.

LOS ALAMOS, NEW MEXICO

In 2012, as we were exploring the Bandelier National Monument in New Mexico, we found out that the Manhattan Project in Los Alamos was just wenty minutes away. So we took a little detour and went to see what has now become the third unit of the Manhattan Project National Historical Park. It was then its central design and production facility, codenamed "Site Y.".

Just like for the plutonium production facility, it was decided that this central facility should be in a remote, but central, location separate from Oak Ridge. Robert Oppenheimer, the nuclear physicist who designed the nuclear bombs, recommended that it should be somewhere near Albuquerque where he had a ranch. He was impressed with the vicinity of the Los Alamos Ranch School because the views of the Sangre de Cristo Mountains would be inspiring for the scientists who would work on the project.

That is where a team of scientists led by him, including Enrico Fermi, designed and built the atom bombs. We delighted in seeing the cottages on Bath Tub Row where they lived, the only homes in the facility with bath tubs. General Leslie R. Groves took charge of building and maintaining the infrastructure while the scientists pondered the imponderables.

On July 16, 1945 the first ever atomic bomb was tested and detonated at Trinity Site, southwest of Albuquerque, at New Mexico's Alamogordo Bombing and Gunnery Range. Unfortunately that site was only open two days a year so we were not able to see it. Today, visits to the site are sponsored by the Alamogordo Chamber of Commerce on the first Saturdays of April and October. The rest of the year the site is closed to the public because it lies within the impact zone for missiles fired.

The rest is history. Little Boy, the uranium weapon, was dropped in Hiroshima on August 6, 1945; and three days later, Fat Man, the plutonium bomb, was dropped on Nagasaki. That ended WWII, preventing the loss of countless lives had the hostilities lasted for more months and years. The Bradbury Science Museum in the Los Alamos National Laboratory tells the whole story and houses full-size models of the two bombs.

In the immediate postwar years, the Manhattan Project conducted weapons testing, developed new weapons, supported medical research into radiology and laid the foundations for the nuclear Navy. It maintained control over American atomic weapons research and production until the formation of the United States

Atomic Energy Commission in January 1947. Finally, its pivotal role promoted the development of the current network of National Laboratories.

These laboratories now number seventeen and are at the fore-front of scientific research and development, some of which are found nowhere else in the world. The Los Alamos National Laboratory that designed and finally assembled the bombs still operates today as part of the network. One of them, Lawrence Livermore National Laboratory, is very near my daughter's home so we have also visited that laboratory. We would like to visit more. It is so interesting and inspiring to see why and how the US was and continues to be at the forefront of the scientific challenges of the modern world.

10

UTILIZING TECHNOLOGY ON THE GO

§

Technology is the sum total of state-of-the-art means (specific methods, materials, and devices) used to solve today's practical problems. Today's means include hardware, software, internet, social media, etc. The practical problems of cruising in an RV are 1) reducing load on the RV to minimize fuel expense; 2) getting around new places on unfamiliar roads, 3) being prepared for all kinds of conditions (no power, getting stranded, etc.); 4) staying in contact with others; and 5) other needs like documentation, entertainment, cooking, etc.. This post gives you a scan of general purpose gadgets and the special RV technologies we learned to use on the go.

GENERAL PURPOSE GADGETS

Some of the general purpose gadgets we carried in our RV included high-powered, lightweight laptops, a GPS with real time traffic information, the latest in smartphones with mobile Hotspot, a Kindle reader, a tablet, his and hers iPods, a digital camera, and smart TVs.

This is a lot of processing power. We used the laptop and tablet for keeping and updating many digital files, banking and paying bills, writing posts, processing photos, and emailing and video-chatting with family. The Kindle held about fifty-odd books and magazines for Bill and me. And our smartphones, besides being our phones, were equipped with a Mobile Hotspot, became our PDAs (personal digital assistants), and served as back-up cameras. In addition, our iPods have faithfully kept all the music we treasure.

The GPS had built-in guides to the type of food we craved at the moment, the local attraction we did not want to miss, the nearest gas station, and other necessities of being in a new location. Together with the smartphones, we had all we needed to get to wherever we wanted to go. Powered by satellite transmission, the GPS never failed us, as long as it was updated——, and we had a lifetime update feature.

Cameras became very important, too. I loved my Nikon DSLR. Photos I took with it won many awards. But it was so bulky I had always asked Bill to carry it for me. Knowing how I had gotten to love photography, Bill gifted me with the Sony Mirrorless Camera, the newest thing in cameras. It is the size of a point and shoot camera, but has the power of a DSLR. Recently, my children even gifted me with an expensive camera drone that gives unique panoramic shots from up above. How I wish I had it when we were fulltime RVing. Now it is the problem of storing photos that has taken center stage. Fortunately, Google Photos helps me organize and keep all my phone photos in the cloud, for free. And I already have several external hard drives with terra bytes of capacity and USB micro cards with gigabytes.

Presently, we have added a device that we can no longer do without. Aside from keeping track of the number of steps and calories burned, our Fitbits record how we sleep—how much REM, deep or light sleep we had the previous night, how many hours awake and asleep—and our vitals like pulse rate and oxygen saturation of our blood—that help us keep track of things required for healthy living.

SPECIAL PURPOSE TECHNOLOGY

Perhaps I should include my chip-based small karaoke system (yes!) and a combo microwave/oven/crisper here. The Ziller karaoke system is an Asian invention. Karaoke music is kept in microchips and a small portable unit houses them so I could select the songs I want to sing from any of the dual microphone units that came along with it. And my combo microwave/oven/crisper, through the flick of a switch, did what I wanted it to do.

Our home on wheels also utilized plenty of special RV technology. Its systems were mostly satellite-based so that things could still be operable however remote a place we were in. There were different kinds of systems available for different kinds of situations. And the devices were more compact than those used in regular homes.

Let us take power for instance. On the road or while we were dry camping, the refrigerator ran on LPG. Parked at a full-hookup campground, it drew power, like all other appliances and lights, from a 30 or 50 amp circuit—we prefer 50 because we had included everything a home needs, including a washer/dryer. While dry camping, lights were run by house batteries while the generator ran all the other heavy drawers such as the furnace, air-conditioning, microwave/oven, washer/dryer, and even my hair dryer.

Plumbing ran on three tank systems. We could hook up to city water or store it in a "fresh water" tank underneath the RV. The "grey water" tank held the water from the sinks, shower, and washing machine/dryer combo. The "black water" tank held, you guessed it, everything from the toilet. Bill made sure they were all drained and flushed completely and regularly. Most campgrounds have hookups for filling up fresh water, or draining the grey and the black. When they don't—like when we parked at a Walmart or a rest area for a night or just camped by the side of a river as we did on the road to the Arctic Circle—we had to look for public or for pay stations afterward. For the "black water," there is an option of using blue boys or portable suction devices. Luckily, we never had to use them.

Even with our second RV, we did not install solar panels. We loved our satellite In-motion dish which enabled me to watch TV while Bill was driving. He knew I would be grumpy if I could not watch a major tennis match of Nadal's whenever it happened. And then, consider this: driving a 37.5-foot Class A towing a compact car meant a total of about fifty-two to fifty three feet in length. Backing up could have been very tricky. So our RV had a large TV monitor system that helped Bill. And the towing system—Blue Ox was the brand we used—could readily be set up in a Saturn. It was too bad those cars have gone out of production. We never had the opportunity to use the short-wave radio, though.

There have been new technologies, too, since our RVing days. The Internet of Things (IoT) is the network of physical devices, vehicles, home appliances and other items embedded with electronics, software, sensors, etc., which enable them to connect and exchange data with other objects within the Internet. This technology is exploding because it enables many useful things: smart people, smart grids, virtual power plants, smart homes, intelligent transportation, and even smart cities. Alexa is the most elementary form, activating some of the things we have at home via voice recognition. We would have loved one on the road. Then I could have instructed my oven/microwave/crisper to bake/heat/broil. Cool.

After eight years of RVing and in the four more years following, we have many devices we no longer can do without while traveling. The laptop I use is more powerful than any I have used before and yet is the lightest and smallest of them all. The drone is my latest toy. And we charge our phones by just setting them on things that look like simple coasters.

Bill and I are not early adopters but we certainly utilize technology as much as possible. In our mobile lifestyle, technology has become our slave. Actually, it is Bill who introduces new things to me. Often, I do not know how to operate some of them until he teaches me how. I like to say my mechanical IQ is almost zero; Bill says I just want him to do things for me.

11

Traveling Light in an RV

B y definition, you cannot travel light in an RV. How can you travel light when you are, in fact, taking your whole home with you? But that is precisely why traveling as light as possible in an RV is even more crucial. In fact, tackling this subject led us to the one real secret to traveling light whatever the mode of travel you choose to take.

Our RV had about 350 square feet of living space when parked, the size of a standard hotel room. And that includes the bathroom suite. We tried to not add much to its 20,000-pound weight. Living in our moving home for eight years taught us how to keep our every-day needs to a bare minimum. The high cost of fuel was the biggest driving factor.

Actually, we were both already going down the "light" road. When I came to America, I had completely downsized to just two suitcases and a *Balikbayan* (returning resident) Box. Initially, I lived in a room at my daughter's home in Seattle. Soon I was teaching at three institutions of higher learning and bought my own two-bedroom condo. I continued my minimalist lifestyle which had started in Manila, really. I had raised my children in a cozy three-bedroom condo in a high rise tower, just to keep things simple for this single parent. When Bill's second marriage ended, he had bought a duplex, downsized to one of the units, and rented the other out.

When we got married, Bill moved into my condo and ended up renting out the unit he had lived in, too. Soon after, he sold his business and we both retired. We sold most of our stuff on Craigslist and three-yard sales and packed what we needed into our 24-ft. Class B motorhome. We left some boxes in two storage locations: my daughter's garage and the external storage unit of my condo. When we bought our 37.5-foot Class A motorhome, we transferred all that we owned to the big rig and gave away big items to our children. That brought us down to our bare necessities. The question was how to maintain this barest minimum?

THE MATTER OF CLOTHES

Clothes can be the most creeping weight culprit. Bill always said "I've got too many shirts" every time I saw one hanging on a store's rack that looked like it would be great for him. When I found out that high pressure and extreme temperature, whether hot or cold, caused a flare-up of hives, I changed my dress size to large and donated to Goodwill my entire small/medium-sized wardrobe. Recently, I have changed back to medium and made another trip to Goodwill to get rid of my large-sized clothes. When I was little and we were living in the slums of Manila, I had been used to just a few pieces of clothing. I preferred tops and bottoms which I mixed and matched to create a variety of looks. In fact, I had a matrix pasted on to my cabinet which presented all the possible combinations, lest I forget.

THE CASE OF PAPER

Paper adds a lot of pounds, too. As much as possible, we gave up physical books and magazines and limited ourselves to the Kindle and phones instead. Most of our files were converted to electronic format. We kept only those original documents that need to be presented, like passports, birth and marriage certificates, divorce/annulment papers, etc. At some point, we also got our health records into e-patient systems. Even my recipes were kept in two electronic folders. And most photos were scanned, except those with sentimental value.

THE RV KITCHEN REVISITED

Kitchen items can be the heaviest of all. We limited our silver and dinnerware to a service for four and no more. When we had more guests—the RV seats ten inside, plus more outside—we used disposables. Cooking pots were kept in just three sizes-small, medium, and large; frying pans just two, small and medium. But we did have a small slow cooker and microwaveable rice cooker. Bill made do with a French Press, since a coffee machine would have had such a large footprint on our tiny counter space. The small pantry also carried only the bare necessities. And the refrigerator held only a week's worth of food. The microwave and convection oven were in one convertible unit. But, as with many of you, our mug collection kept on growing; and my spice drawer was always too full since I love to cook cuisine from all over the world.

THE RV BATHROOM MAKEOVER

However, I was not as good with the bathroom. Bill kept his toiletries to the minimum. Linens and towels were good for only four people: Bill, me, and two guests. The problem was that my supply of soap, shampoo, conditioner, body lotion, tissue packet, etc. from places we had stayed had grown to be mountains. But now I have put those to good use in what I call a Ziplock Ministry. Into a medium-sized Ziplock bag I put soap, shampoo, and tissue packet from my collection, and add a small toothbrush with a small tube of toothpaste and a pack of crackers with a small can of Vienna sausage. We distribute these to homeless persons we encounter on the road. But, as travelers, we continued to build stocks of them so we will proceed to donate them in bulk to institutions from now on.

OTHER THINGS CONSIDERED ESSENTIAL

In storage bins under the RV, we kept a small portable fire pit (for sitting out even on cold nights), a small barbeque grill, foldable outdoor table and four chairs, two suitcases and two carry-ons for trips elsewhere, Bill's fishing, tennis, and golf gear, and a small ladder. Inside the RV, we carried a DVD player, a small microchip-based Ziller karaoke system, 32-inch and 15-inch TVs, a satellite dish, two iPod players, a laptop, and a Tablet. We also had a small space heater, a small electric fan, and a small vacuum cleaner. Our bed was Queen-size, and we also had a small washer/dryer combo. These are things we considered basic necessities; yes, including the karaoke machine.

During our eight years of RVing, we learned to live with the barest essentials. As a result, even when we transferred to the 1,200 sq. ft. home at Viewpoint, we did not even fill half of our closets, cabinets, and storage spaces (even up to now, three years later). Now we pack only one carry-on for a trip of several days, a carry-on each for more than a week, a checked-in bag and two carry-ons for a month, and two checked-in bags and two carry-ons for three months. The lessons of traveling light in an RV have been extended to something more fundamental. And that is the one real secret to traveling light: living light.

12

OVERHAULING CAROL

§

To overhaul means: to take apart in order to examine and repair, if necessary. I may not be a piece of machinery—though many in my past life in the Philippines said I was close to being one—but this is how Bill's brother-in-law Jack, an engineer and husband of Bill's only sibling and sister, Rosemary, suggested I title this piece.

We visited them in Kansas in the middle of our RVing years. He laid out hook-ups for our RV in their driveway, so for two and a half months, we were neighbors. We have visited them many times before but this was the best. I finally got the chance to be over-hauled and the siblings lived their early years all over again. I just hoped we didn't wear thin their hospitality

This is the main disadvantage of the full time RV cruising life-style that we clearly did not foresee: inconsistent health care. I have talked about ways to mitigate the disadvantage of not being close to family and friends, but with inconsistent healthcare, especially with advancing age, when the health risks of yesterday turn into the health issues of today, there is no mitigation. The best way to address health issues is prevention.

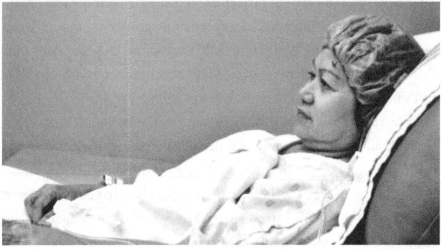

Our lifestyle had us bouncing around North America making six cross-continental runs in just a little more than four years. It's bad enough that we had grown older; it is worse we did not have a family physician who knew our history, continued to see us, and kept our records. Bill contracted pneumonia in Mexico, had arthroscopic surgery in Indiana/Ohio, suffered a heart attack in Florida, and experienced blood clots in his right knee in Colorado.

We often joke about how major but easy and few Bill's ailments are and how mine are irritatingly chronic, hard to diagnose, and harder to cure. I have only talked about the recurring hives and persistent GERD and had kept silent about the others, hoping they would simply go away. So Bill decided that we would stay put at his sister's place for however long it took to take advantage of the good doctors they had locally.

TENDONITIS

A couple of days before we arrived at their home in Pittsburg, Kansas, I had hurt my right wrist. Bill alleges it was because of four to eight hours a day of incessant thumping on the computer keyboard: blogging, surfing, Facebooking, emailing, uploading and editing photos and creating albums, and WWF (Words with Friends). It was painful, but a simple steroid injection by Rosemary's orthopedic doctor freed me of the wrist brace I had been wearing for months.

PLANTAR FASCIITIS

No, I didn't use my feet for my computer work, but I did suffer from plantar fasciitis, too. Bill said it was most probably because I had been wearing cheap shoes. I rejected steroid injections into my feet but the couple's podiatrist recommended in-soles for my footwear. I also started to exercise with foot rollers and still use them from time to time. What a relief they have given me! And I have heeded Bill's admonition. I have changed to shoe brands that are known to be great for the feet. I no longer look at the price, or I will never buy them.

DENTAL CARE

Bill was not happy about the dental care I had experienced with my #5 (post-incisor tooth). It had hurt after our wedding and a dental clinic in Kent, Washington did a root canal. When I got to the Philippines in 2009, my dentist thought I had better see an endodontist. So she referred us to one of only two such dentists in the country, who performed another root canal on the tooth. Well, I don't think that went well. The filling placed after the procedures kept on falling out. In fact, it was redone three times, twice in the US and another time in the Philippines. In Pittsburg, I was referred to an oral and maxillofacial surgeon, who decided that the tooth should no longer be saved, and extracted it.

CHRONIC HIVES

The day Bill returned from the hospital after his heart attack, I experienced sciatica. Excruciating pain left me to be cared for by Bill, who was himself just recovering. A week later it was replaced by aggressive hives. Four doctors and two years later, I still had them. And we were still dazed and confused. In Pittsburg, Jack's family physician gave me an aggressive dose of non-sedating anti-allergy medication. And I became free of hives, except for one or two that appeared once in a while. Over time, they all disappeared.

CATARACT SURGERY

I had been wearing glasses since grade school due to aggressive myopia. My study habits did not help at all. In 1997 I was one of the very first beneficiaries of laser eye surgery in the Philippines. Less than ten years after, however, my vision started to deteriorate again. From 2009-2011, our first two years of RVing, I needed new prescription lenses every six months. Jack's ophthalmologist recommended an eye surgeon, and both prescribed cataract surgery on both eyes. Now I carry two cards for my implants. After the surgery, I woke up every morning without having to look for my glasses (except when I needed to read or look smart). Bill survived the fear that I would finally see how he really looks with my much-improved vision.

POSSIBILITY OF BREAST CANCER

But, guess what the doctors in Pittsburg discovered was my biggest health issue? A mammogram detected a seven-mm mass on my right breast. An ultrasound was done, then the physical examination. They instructed me to have another mammogram done in another three months to see if the mass had grown so a biopsy could be done to test for malignancy. The process of overhauling apparently would not be completed in Pittsburg. Later, after two more biennial checks and two mass-excisions, I finally went back to regular annual mammograms. Still, our stay with Jack and Rosemary had started and almost completed the overhaul process; and for all intents and purposes, I am now a bionic woman.

What is most significant is that we learned full time RVing should not be carried to the extreme we did at our age. It was certainly possible to fulltime without being constantly on the move, as we had done. Our next travel patterns will feature settling down in a regular home, visiting family, friends, and other destinations but also staying put several months a year. We now think there is wisdom in having roots; even if, as Bill says, we are not trees.

13

LOOKING FOR A BASE
IN ARIZONA

§

We have settled in Arizona but how did we come to select the state? Actually, we had spent seven months in Florida and loved it, but it was the farthest from our children. Even if we had dreamed of settling there, we had to eliminate it from our options. Southern California may have been ideal, too, especially because it is a haven for Filipinos. But California had (and still has) such a high cost of living. It would not have been smart to choose it. And because we were RVing, we actually had the chance to live all around Arizona for three months. That's what we did and how we came up with a truly informed decision.

NORTHEASTERN ARIZONA

To explore this area, we based our RV at the Verde Valley RV Resort that was nestled in the lower valley and cooler than the business district of Cottonwood, Arizona. This town had a population of 11,000 and was only fifteen minutes away from our base. It is also less than two hours from Phoenix with many interesting attractions around it.

Just ten minutes away was Montezuma Castle, an elaborate five-story 100-room cliff dwelling built in 1100 AD, standing 100 feet above the valley and etched into a rock. Nearby Montezuma Well, on the other hand, had been a natural sinkhole, containing over fifteen million gallons of water, replenished every day with one and a half million gallons of water that unbelievably drain from the surrounding dry and arid land. Eleven minutes from Cottonwood was Tuzigoot National Monument, a village built between 1125 and 1400 AD crowning the summit of a ridge that rises 120 feet from the valley floor. Up the hill is the little town of Jerome, Arizona (population almost 500), a former mining town that still has THE grand old mansion of its heyday, the original jail, and a museum of the town history. It is now a little touristy area of lodging, shops, and eateries just twenty minutes away.

Northwest of Cottonwood, just 30 minutes away, is the beautiful city of Sedona. It was even smaller in population than Cottonwood. But imagine a city embedded in what should be a national park of outstanding red rock formations: Cathedral Rock (the icon), Linus and Lucy, Coffee Pot, Bell, Courthouse, etc. We even had the good fortune of getting to the Schnebly Hill Vista Point at sundown for a complete overlook of the city and all the rocks. The Chapel of the Holy Cross, on a thousand-foot high rock wall, soaring ninety more feet into the air, offered a great place for contemplation.

Going farther north, only an hour away, is the bigger city of Flagstaff (population 60,000). Its Old Historic District has an establishment that features a timer countdown to New Year's —a giant pine cone attached to its roof—just like New York City's Times Square. Flagstaff is surrounded by three National Monuments. Sun Crater Volcano National Monument is a thousand foot-high cinder cone created by an eruption between 1040 and 1100 AD that totally changed the landscape into the 600 hills and mountains of northern Arizona. It must also have changed the lives of the Ancient

CAROLINA ESGUERRA COLBORN

Puebloans that lived at the nearby 35,000 acres of the Wupatki National Monument, featuring twenty-nine continuing structures of an estimated 12,000 pueblos. And then there is the Walnut Canyon National Monument with cliff dwellings of the Sinaguas carved into the canyon's natural recesses, about three meters deep, between 1125 and 1250 AD.

But the grandest of them all is the Grand Canyon National Park whose East Rim is just two hours and a half north of Cottonwood. There is a Watchtower that provided the best vista of the Desert View. Following the Canyon Rim Road, we also reached the South Rim (Mather Point) ten miles west in just another half hour, stopping at almost every overlook, each providing yet another majestic view. The Grand Canyon Village at the South Rim has a huge Visitor Center, lots of shopping areas, and dining and lodging choices.

Northeastern Arizona was truly spectacular. It would have been great to host the many visitors who want to see this part of the state blessed by many natural landmarks and Native American historic sites. But we did not think Cottonwood, Sedona, or Flagstaff would make the finals in our selection process, however. It was just November and it was already a little cooler than we would like our neighborhood to be. I could just imagine what it would be in winter. Besides, I was really still a big city girl. Perhaps Phoenix or Tucson, our next two visits would win in the end. We could just take our guests to tour this northeastern part from a more southern base.

PHOENIX

Phoenix is the fifth largest city in the US, with a population of 1.6 million (SMSA, six million), following Houston, Chicago, LA, and New York. Because of relatively warm and sunny winters, its suburbs are populated by many good RV parks. We particularly liked the Viewpoint RV and Golf Resort that surrounded two golf courses, ten tennis and ten pickle ball courts, a ball field, a bar/grille and many other amenities for its 1,900 sites, a third of them reserved for RVs, the rest containing park models and now manufactured homes.

Superstition Mountains hovered in the distance at the Resort. They are located beyond Apache Junction, a Phoenix burb, just next to Viewpoint. On the Apache Trail, we found unusually scenic sites; even an Elvis Chapel at the Superstition Visitor Center and Museum. The Chapel was blasted in one of the movies he made, but it had been restored for tourism. Part of the magic was the Goldfield Ghost Town, where they reenacted a 'gunfight' every afternoon during peak season. Three lakes surround the Trail and Tortilla Flats (population, six) is its last surviving stagecoach stop that has a great country store and restaurant.

I was actually surprised to find the Phoenix metropolitan area pretty. I'd thought it was just a huge desert. The Desert Botanical Garden offers unusual greenery that has adapted to an otherwise arid land. We climbed to the Hole in the Rock nearby, and it was as entertaining to look up to the blue sky from the Hole as down to the valley below. From there we had great views of Hunt's Tomb. Hunt was a best-loved first governor of the state who served for an astounding seven terms. Dobbins' Lookout on South Mountain offered an aerial city view.

There is a small cityscape of tall buildings because the area is widely spread out. There was just that much desert land. Right at the center is Pueblo Grande, the Hohokam Ruins that thrived from 900 BC to 1450 AD, much like Chaco Canyon or Taos Pueblo in New Mexico and Wupatki in Flagstaff. The Spanish influence has also remained strong. Many unique architectural sites also surround downtown Phoenix: the Tovrea Castle, looking like a huge wedding cake; the Mystery Castle, a Dad's interpretation of his daughter's fantasy; Wrigley Mansion, part of the chewing gum magnate's legacy; and Taliesin West, the companion masterpiece of Frank Lloyd Wright's Taliesin East in Wisconsin.

TUCSON

From everything we heard about city size, climate during winter months, and other criteria, Tucson had gone to the top of our list. Excited, we went to inspect six RV Resorts and chose to stay at the biggest one with 1,500 sites, Voyager RV Resort. It had a motel on site for guests plus a grocery store and all the standard amenities including a golf course, tennis and pickle ball courts, a clubhouse, a pool and hot tub, a restaurant, and plenty of clubs to choose from. But they were not as many, or as grand as the ones in Viewpoint in Phoenix.

Tucson, with a population more than half a million (SMSA of almost a million) is a modern metropolis already, with the demographics of what the US will be in 2050 (non-Hispanic whites as a minority). Sentinel Peak is an easy-to-access vantage point for an aerial view of the city. Two districts of the Saguaro National Park—that conserve fine tracts of the Sonoran Desert with the Tucson Mountains in the west and the Rincon Mountains in the east—surround the city. The park gets its name from the large cactus native to the region, the largest of which can be seventy-five feet tall and ten feet wide.

The University of Arizona is located in Tucson and operates the only Biosphere2 on the planet, designed to mimic Biosphere 1 (the earth). It had been an amazing venture, started in the late 1980s by the Texas billionaire Edward Bass who put in $250M to create this infrastructure with five different ecological systems: tropical rainforest, savannah, marshland, ocean, and desert. In the early 1990s, eight Biospherians (four women and four men) lived there for two years and learned much about human ecology. The University of Arizona has recently expanded it to include LEO (Landscape Evolution Observatory). The main thrust today is to study the conservation of water on earth, one of the key ingredients of life and a scarce resource in the desert.

The influence of the Spanish and Native Americans was still very evident in many places in Tucson. The Mission San Javier del Bac is a beautiful white adobe church, one of two notable churches in honor of St. Francis Xavier. It was founded in 1692 and is internationally recognized as the finest example of Spanish Colonial architecture in the US, highly evident in the rough but gilded altars and statuary. We heard mass there on his Feast Day, Dec. 2, and witnessed men happily lighting ground fireworks, like New Year's in Manila. And what a delicious lunch we had that day, with all the Mexican/Indian tiendas selling hot local fry bread with carne de seca. We were also privileged to hear Christmas Eve Mass there last year enroute to Mexico.

Other fine churches are the Cathedral of St. Augustine, completed in 1868, housing the Diocese. Another charming chapel, the Chapel of San Pedro, belonging to the Old Fort Lowell Neighborhood Association, is frequently used for weddings and belongs on the National Register of Historic Places. South of Tucson is the Tucumcacori Mission, built in 1691. It was the first of the trail of missions built by the Spanish Anza that continued on to California. We also visited Barrio Historico which featured many old colorful adobe homes with cacti growing around their perimeters.

Tucson would also be a great base for interesting small towns, most notably Tombstone where the Battle of the OK Corral is reenacted regularly. Tubac, famous for its fine furniture and craft making, has thousands of lights marking its Iluminaria Night on Dec. 7 & 8 every year. Finally, Bisbee was a rich mining town of old and the setting of several mystery novels of renowned author J.A. Jance.

Tucson was a definite contender, alongside Phoenix. It is a big enough city, and the weather is even better than Phoenix (lower by five degrees). There are good hospitals and educational institutions; cheap Mexican goods and more authentic Mexican cuisine are more easily available; and taxes are lower. But we decided to suspend our decision until we finished visiting the last candidate, Yuma.

YUMA

We actually reached Yuma, very near the Mexican border, close to Christmas day. We loved the RVs abundantly decorated for the season at our chosen campground, Yuma Lakes Resort. On Christmas Eve, Bill and I had our *noche Buena* and the opening of gifts and stocking stuffers. On Christmas day the folks of the campground provided everything, and we just had to bring sides or dessert. It was a sumptuous Christmas Day lunch but, as usual, we didn't win any of the raffle prizes; not even as the best decorated RV (I had a small, brilliant Christmas lantern called a *parol* in the Philippines at the center of radiating Christmas lights).

Yuma has a population of 100,000, which increases to 200,000 in winter time due to the influx of snow birders. The valley is a huge agricultural area with acres upon acres of cauliflower, lettuce, and green and purple cabbages. Downtown is just like any other city with its chain stores in malls, theaters, restaurants, fast food outlets, and, of course, Walmart.

But the best part of Yuma is that it is only eight miles from the Mexican border. Since our campground was only nine miles from the center of Yuma, Mexico was just 25 minutes from where our RV was parked. We literally walked to the town of Los Algodones, after parking our Saturn at a lot near the Port of Entry.

The Mexican town is mainly four whole blocks of dental, optical and medical clinics, pharmacies, and liquor stores. That is where Yuma snow birders fill their needs for a song. The sidewalks and plaza were filled with vendors of Mexican goods that are "almost free." When we walked to the Port of Entry of Andrade, we were asked what we were bringing into the US. We said: two sterling silver necklace/bracelet sets, three sterling silver Omega fashion necklaces, three sets of sterling silver earrings, three big stylish heavy ponchos, one giant Don Julio tequila bottle, and two pouches of authentic Mexican flour tortillas, all for only $200.

We also had our fill of cheap authentic Mexican food: *carne asada tampiquena* consisting of *chili relleno*, cheese *enchilada*, steak, and beans, making a very colorful plate for brunch. For an early dinner we had chicken *fajitas* and margaritas at the Paraiso, where we had a big fiesta with Mariachis playing "cowboy" and Mexican songs. We danced with others from Yuma, doing rock and roll, cha-cha and everything in between and a group was wearing t-shirts with the words "We partied in Los Algodones!"

But we did not really see ourselves being happy in Yuma and Los Algodones for long. It was too small a metropolis for a big-city girl like me. Options would get fewer as weeks rolled by. In fact, we were supposed to stay for two weeks but we cut our stay to just five days, with a day in Mexico to boot. In other words, it ended up to be a decision between Phoenix and Tucson.

That question was decided by just one factor. Phoenix is home to Arizona's Phoenix Sky Harbor International Airport. For perennial travelers like us, and with children spread across four states and two other countries, a hub like Phoenix would be hugely attractive. We comforted ourselves with the fact that our favorites around Tucson, Cottonwood, and Yuma would all be easy to get to. We promise not to disappoint our guests and visitors.

14

WHAT WE LEARNED FROM EIGHT YEARS OF RVING

Note: This was an article I wrote for and published by TravelAwaits.

Our wedding on a private cruise ship led us directly into a cruising lifestyle—just not on the water. Our honeymoon became eight years of North American travels in an RV. After we began to spend winters in Arizona, I got to work on my first book, *Carolina: Cruising,* about the adventure. It includes not only my immigration and love story but also RVing lessons. This article highlights the most memorable ones.

CHOOSING THE RIGHT RV MAKES ALL THE DIFFERENCE

The first problem we faced as we were starting our new on-the-road lifestyle was choosing what RV to buy. We settled on a used 24-foot Class B motorhome for $10,000. I called our RV "Star." She had enough storage space, and I appreciated that the bedroom/

bathroom could be closed off from the living/driving areas. We bought for her a companion I called "Vino," a cute blue scooter.

Star and Vino took us from Seattle to Calgary, up through the Alaska Highway, around Alaska and the Arctic Circle, down along the North American West Coast, into Mexico, then across the Gulf States and into all of Florida. Our first Christmas away from home was spent in Orlando, Florida. Fuel efficiency, easy maneuverability, and low initial investment—those were the criteria we used in choosing the Star-and-Vino tandem. It was perfect for our first eight months of RVing.

FINDING THE RIGHT WAY TO RV

There was one drawback to all our driving around on our extended trip after our wedding: it was somewhat tiring for my husband. We needed to find another way to continue our RVing on a more full-time basis, staying longer in each stop.

Realizing that camping costs were our single biggest expense, not fuel, we bought a membership in a national campground network. This reduced our camping expenses from an average of $15 to less than $5 a night over the next five years. And it was sad, but we eventually had to trade in Star and Vino for a 37.5-foot Class A motorhome with a used compact car for a dinghy. The newlyweds finally had a "home" where they could host guests, stay in resort campgrounds for weeks instead of days, and explore each area extensively and comfortably in a compact car. The new expenses actually resulted in fewer dollars spent.

If you are retired or your career is portable, living this dream is a smart way to travel in North America. However, if you are tied to a job, to family, or constrained by any other reason, you may consider "escaping" on weekends and holidays. Start by transforming your vehicle into a campervan, if suitable, or renting a small RV. You will be thrilled to get to your coveted destinations with the utmost freedom of movement and in today's times, safely.

PLANNING ROUTES

Our campground membership gave us a whole range of options to explore the entirety of the US. Of course, national parks and forests provided a whole additional set of choices, especially with substantial discounts for seniors. It was therefore easy to plan itineraries based on three factors: closeness to attractions or family/friends we wanted to visit, climate, and distance. Generally, we followed the sun and created routes according to a logical sequence of destinations to further save on fuel expenses.

Unfortunately, one time we made a most grievous error. My son-in-law was taking care of our mail, and a hugely important letter did not reach me in time because of successive changes in itinerary. It was for an appointment with the U.S. Commission on Immigration Services in connection with my application for citizenship. When I finally got it, the appointment date in Seattle had already passed. My request to reschedule was granted, but we had a knee-jerk reaction and raced our "home" across the country. It was foolish. We should have stored the RV, flown to the meeting, and flown back to continue our drive up the East Coast. After that experience, we shifted to a professional mail forwarding service and vowed to do a better job of sticking to our planned routes.

BUYING FROM LOCAL STORES AS WELL AS NATIONAL CHAINS

With any used RV, maintenance is an ongoing concern. At first, we used local service providers to help the economies of the towns we passed through. But when our roof sprung a leak in Spokane, Washington, no local service company wanted to take on such a big job. We hesitated to, because it was more expensive, but had to have the repairs done by a branch of Camping World, a national chain. After the job was finished, we had to leave right away to meet my daughter and her family at Glacier National Park. Unfortunately, when it rained again, once we were in Chicago, we found out that there was still a slight leak. But we heaved a sigh of relief because the chain had an outlet there, one of its 120 branches in thirty-six states. The job was completed to our satisfaction in Illinois.

The value of national chains is also true for the company to choose for roadside assistance. We dealt with flat tires twice—once in an isolated canyon in Utah, and later in the middle of a busy interstate highway approaching Kentucky from Ohio. It was good Bill maintained a membership in Good Sam, a great roadside assistance service. Help arrived in under an hour for both instances. There was another scary time when my husband's heart medication ran out. That would have been a crisis in the Philippines, where I grew up. But in the US, it was very easy to transfer his prescription to the nearby branch of Walgreens, the nationwide pharmacy we patronized at the time.

Using national chains gave us a lot of flexibility. The only thing we wished for that was not (and still not, I believe) available was a national fishing license. However, we had great fun buying food, crafts, arts, and other small items at Farmers' Markets, local art dealers, and other outlets, supporting the local economy in the process.

Building Healthcare into Your Plans

That brings us to the last lesson which we learned late in the game. Early into our RVing, my new groom suffered a minor heart attack. It was such a stressful situation for us both. As a result, chronic hives kept me company for months. When he developed a blood clot behind his right knee, the hives were replaced by intense bouts of acid reflux. Our health issues did not stop there. We should have returned once a year to a place — somewhere central — where a regular physician, dentist, and ophthalmologist could have taken care of us. We had totally neglected preventive care, given all the travel excitement.

Still, RVing is an experience people should have at least once in their lifetime, whether as fulltime RVers like we were, for shorter weekend escapes, or for extended vacations. It is simply the most liberating mode of travel. And now, with Covid-19, it is even the safest. You have total control of how clean your quarters are and keeping it open only to your safe bubble.

15

Discovering America, the Beautiful

§

The lesson that will linger the longest in our hearts is the beauty of America we saw first-hand: her natural grandeur, her significant places of history, and the unrivalled diversity of her people. It didn't take long after we started RVing before I began humming that beloved American Scout Song, *America the Beautiful.*

> O beautiful for spacious skies,
> For amber waves of grain,
> For purple mountain majesties,
> Above thy fruited plain.

The lyrics of this Scout Song will ring true for many centuries to come because the US protects her natural beauty and heritage like no other country in the world. As of 2015, 25,800 properties, comprising fourteen percent of the country's total land area, are protected. The number constitutes ten percent of the world's total conserved area even if the US is less than two percent of the world's total land area. The extent of protection will ensure that not only Americans will enjoy the country's best for a long, long time but also those who visit our land from all parts of the world.

The US performs this great conservation effort at different levels of government. Federal, state, tribal, and local authorities manage this important function. All fifty states participate, together with the following federal agencies that are in the forefront:

National Landscape Conservation System (Bureau
   of Land Management Special Areas)
National Park Service
National Wild and Scenic Rivers System
National Wildlife Refuge System
U.S. Army Corps of Engineers
U.S. Forest Service
U.S. Marine Protected Areas

There are many designations used for these protected areas; the major two among them are national parks and national monuments. Of fifty-nine national parks and one hundred twenty-two national monuments, Bill and I have visited thirty-two and thirty-one, respectively. We also have visited one hundred seven other protected areas such as national historical parks, national historic sites, etc. And we do not include in our count state and regional conservation areas. As a matter of fact, we also visited the protected areas of Canada and Mexico. I have written about most of those we have visited in my first book, *Carolina: Cruising.*

Bill and I thought that we should rank all those we have seen; it is a question we are asked all the time. Information like this can help you plan itineraries. We used only one criterion that stood out from their very definitions. For National Parks, we used "outstanding natural beauty." For National Monuments, on the other hand, we used "exemplary resource because of natural or historical significance." It is interesting to note that the Grand Canyon was a national monument until 1908 first before the government elevated its status to a national park in 1919.

OUR TOP NATIONAL PARKS AND MONUMENTS

Bill and I had the same rankings for the top three national parks, differed slightly about the next three, but disagreed vehemently on the next four. I am sure most of you who have seen them will agree with the rankings. For those who have not been to one or more of them, you should really put them in your bucket lists. We have agreed on the following six:

Grand Canyon in Arizona
Yosemite in California
Yellowstone in Wyoming and Montana
Denali in Alaska
Crater Lake in Oregon
Haleakala in Hawaii

The same thing happened for national monuments. We had almost identical rankings for the top five and differed slightly on the sixth but greatly on the next four. Just like for national parks, if you have not been to one or more of these, please put them on your lists together with those above. Here are the national monuments we chose as our Top Six:

Statue of Liberty in New York
Mt. Rushmore in South Dakota
Chaco Culture in New Mexico
Giant Sequoia in California
Hanford Reach in Washington
Effigy Mounds in Iowa

No one will regret taking the time to go to these twelve protected areas. Any extended travel plan for visiting the US should try to include these twelve. They will all leave you with the lasting impression that America is indeed not only beautiful from the Atlantic to the Pacific, but also steeped in history from its beginnings as a land of Native Americans to its current status as a world leader. They should leave you with the same sentiments they left me: that America deserves unity and brotherhood, instead of the divisiveness and hatred that are spreading today. We hope the message of the last paragraph of the classic Scout Song will ring louder and truer still:

America! America!
God shed his grace on thee
And crown thy good with brotherhood
From sea to shining sea!

OUR TOP STATES AND METROPOLITAN AREAS

Our cruising in RVs also took us to forty-nine American states, so Bill and I also agreed to rank our Top Ten states and cities to visit or live in. This can help in building itineraries but also in choosing where to stay longer for a specific season, or where to settle whenever one gets the chance to do so. This was trickier, so we first had to agree on the criteria to be used. Then we developed a decision matrix to make our final selection.

We had three criteria: things to see, places to eat, and things to do. We voted independently, actually while we were in separate states, he in Idaho helping his son and I in Washington with my daughter. We combined our scores electronically, giving weights to each criterion. Obviously, for the places to visit, things to see was more important; and for places to live in, places to eat and things to do were given greater weights. These are the lists we came up with:

Top Ten States to Visit

1. Arizona
2. Pennsylvania
3. New York
4. Massachusetts
5. Maine
6. California
7. Florida
8. Virginia
9. North Carolina
10. New Mexico

This ranking should tell you that we love history and nature. It also shows why we finally chose to stay in Arizona.

Top Five Metropolitan Areas to Visit as a Winter Haven

1. Tampa, Florida
2. Orlando, Florida
3. Phoenix, Arizona
4. Tucson, Arizona
5. San Diego, California

We loved Florida but, as we have already explained, it is just too far from where our children live. We chose to try Phoenix and became snow birds there for three winters before we chose it for our home base. Now, however, we have moved farther south to Mexico for winter. Of course, when it is winter here, it is summer in Melbourne, Australia where one of my daughters lives. So that's another winter haven.

Top Five Metropolitan Areas to Visit in As a Summer Haven

1. San Francisco, California
2. Seattle, Washington
3. New York City, New York
4. Boston, Massachusetts
5. Philadelphia, Pennsylvania

We left our heart in San Francisco. I am so glad my eldest daughter has decided to move there, so now we vacation with them every year during summer. And, since we were originally a couple from Seattle, we have friends there and all our rental properties are still there. I should also include Calgary, Alberta in Canada, Anchorage, Alaska, Denver, Colorado, and Boise, Idaho as summer havens. Our children have homes there.

Top Five Metropolitan Areas to Live in Year-Round

1. San Diego, California
2. Las Vegas, Nevada
3. Phoenix, Arizona
4. Savannah, Georgia
5. Albuquerque, New Mexico

We should have chosen to settle in San Diego especially because there are so many Filipino communities there but the city (as well as all parts of California) is too expensive to live in. Las Vegas, on the other hand, is too busy for our own good. So we chose to base ourselves in Phoenix during spring and fall, in Mexico during winter, and to visit family during summer. Savannah is in the east, again, too far from where our children live; and Albuquerque is fairly near Phoenix.

PART 2
CHANGES MADE

§

*"The real voyage of discovery consists not in seeking new
landscapes but in having new eyes."*

—— MARCEL PROUST

Travel has transformative powers. It has definitely changed me.
And the changes have been huge. Don't be surprised because
this part has a different structure than the other two. For each story
of change I told, I included one, two or sometimes three vignettes
to help describe it. They are anecdotes that belong to the making
of that change, and are some of my most widely-read and best loved
blog posts.

First, I had little chance of not becoming a wife. My first marriage, to the father of my children, did not last ten years. My second
marriage happened in America to a man from Texas; it lasted only
two. It is good America believes the third time is a charm; I didn't

give up, and stayed. Bill walked into my life when I was about to turn sixty, and last August, we celebrated our twelfth anniversary. RVing gave us the delightful distraction of a seemingly never-ending honeymoon while we were learning to squeeze our two big personalities into the 350 square feet of living space.

When we started to RV, I began to blog to record our travels. I have since become a better writer—I think—and have a decent readership for my blog, have published three books, and have a new hobby as a freelance writer. In fact, I have even become good at taking photos. I don't think I will ever be a professional photographer but they say I have the eye for what makes good pictures. In other words, I have now become more than a writer. I have become a storyteller.

With all the travels, I also have learned the *art* of going from one place to another. I am no longer just a tourist who wanders out of curiosity, bouncing from one spot to another, taking photos to be able to say, "I was there." I have now learned how to explore a new place, immerse in a new way of life, and even go back. And Bill has taught me how to leave my comfort zone once in a while. In fact, we have even gone out of our way to make little pilgrimages.

Aside from becoming a wanderer, writer, and wife, however, there are other facets of Carol that have emerged. Bill gave me such support, for example, that I had another chance at being a better mother. He let me visit my children for weeks, sometimes even months, to cook for them and to take care of their children while they went to work. Bill even shared in the babysitting. And in becoming a better mother, I also became a grandmother to seven grandchildren, experiencing the happiest times with them, and hoping for the bright new world of being a great grandparent. In other words, I finally have the chance and ability to play the role I was deprived of when I was a provider in Manila.

I also stood little chance of not becoming an American. I had applied for American citizenship even before I married Bill. But I strongly believed it should not be just about getting a piece of paper. Against the backdrop of America's beauty, I truly became an American. This particular inner journey was euphoric, at first, until I felt extremely guilty about abandoning my native land. You see, American citizenship meant giving up being a Filipino. And then everything came together when, two years after, I rekindled the Filipino in me and finally became a dual citizen, a Filipino-American.

And the rest came naturally. I began to have a more global sense as we traveled from country to country, adopting other countries as "homes." Actually, Mexico is now our third home, and we spend three months a year there. The UK, Australia, and Canada are countries which my children have chosen to be their own. I have come to adopt them, too, not only because travel has taught me to be open to and accepting of other ways of living, but also because I enjoy a lot of time in them.

I might have had intra-optical lenses replace the cataracts in both eyes and the macular hole in my right eye repaired, but these physical changes are not what I mean when I say I do have new eyes. My past life has been turned upside down. Since the time I came to America at fifty-four, I have been living the last third of my life. I am now a more mature Filipino-American wanderer, writer, and wife; and a better mother, grandmother (hopefully soon, a great-grandmother), and emerging global citizen.

1

FINALLY, BECOMING A WIFE

§

Every summer we do a long road trip to escape the Phoenix sizzle. That is also the time we visit family and celebrate our anniversary somewhere special. This year we had to break the trip into
two short ones because the pandemic did not allow us to visit our
children in Alaska, Canada, and Australia. But it was good we were
able to celebrate our twelfth anniversary in two places.

The first was at the Cliff Lodge of the Snowbird Ski & Summer
Resort in the Cottonwood Canyon of the Wasatch Mountains in
Utah. We were on a road trip to visit Bill's daughter in Denver,
Colorado at the Rocky Mountain National Park. After two weeks
back at home, we took another road trip to Livermore, California
to visit my daughter. And we stopped for the actual week of our
anniversary at the Snow Lake Lodge in Big Bear Lake.

And rightly so, because twelve years is the longest period that I
have been married. I think I should be congratulated, because the
journey toward becoming a wife had not been easy; but some who

know me would congratulate Bill more. In truth, it probably could not have happened if Bill and I were not retired and didn't travel together. That is why we always make it a point to celebrate somewhere special. This year, it was to two places.

My turning point started when my sister passed on from cancer in 2003— without her husband from whom she had been estranged, and without her daughter who died the previous year, also of cancer. I decided I didn't want to die the same way, all alone. When my three children had all graduated from college, had careers of their own, and the two older ones had left the nest, I had to recast my lonely life as an overstressed single parent.

In my first book, I wrote that "I wanted time to cook a little, teach a little, travel a little, write a little, and, yes, love a little." The last one would have been impossible in Manila. The Philippines did not have divorce laws, only a long and costly annulment process although I got lucky when I was given one practically for free when I became a high-ranking government official. Still, it seemed all the good ones had already been taken by the time I turned fifty-four. I decided to wind down my career early. I wanted to face the world with someone by my side.

Less than a year later, I found myself in North America, where two of my three children make their home. It was unfortunate that I had to leave my twenty-four year-old *Bunso* (youngest child) all alone in our Makati home. But I had an eager candidate, a naturopath in Texas I had met on the Net and with whom I had been corresponding while he was trying to help my sister navigate the natural alternatives to a cancer cure. He visited me in Seattle at my eldest daughter's home where I had retreated and was happily babysitting and cooking for the family.

Soon he took me to Texas to be his wife. Unfortunately, the marriage didn't last. He had nursed me back to health; I was down to about 100 pounds when I entered the US. But when I was reenergized and after having driven two road trips from our Texas home—one to the east to visit my sister in Virginia and the other west to visit another sister in California—he felt he had had enough travel. After just two years, I returned to my family to take care of grandkids, first in Calgary, then Seattle. There I was again caught in the web of a driven life. I was doomed. My fate seemed clear. I was not good wife-material.

Enter a new knight in shining armor. He was almost as driven as I was. He had been President and CEO of a national printing solutions company, board director for the Document Management Industry Association of America, a member of the pastoral council of his parish, and an active participant in the speakers' bureau in the Washington chapter of one of the two major political parties.

He was the owner of a printing franchise when, in 2007, we "fashionably" met on the Net. A year later, we married. Soon he sold his business, I resigned all my posts, and we bought an RV. We crossed North America in a whirlwind at first, and crossed the continent four more times in the next three years. I loved every minute of it.

But the RV community is not really diverse. I met only one Asian, one Hispanic couple, and a few African-Americans in all our years of RVing. It was a milieu so distant and different from my homeland. The isolation of the lifestyle was not insurmountable but difficult for the Filipina in me, and I longed for a familiar social support system. In the cozy confines of the RV, changes came as fast as the scenes shifted. And we soon found out that there was absolutely no truth to the throw pillow we bought at the Palm Springs Village Fest that proclaimed, "We get along in our RV 'cuz we have no room to disagree!"

But all couples disagree, about small things and big things. John Gottman in *The Seven Principles for Making Marriage Work* says that sixty-nine per cent of a couple's problems will never go away because most disagreements are rooted in fundamental differences. Dan Wile said it best in his book *After the Honeymoon:* "When choosing a long-term partner... you will inevitably be selecting a particular set of unsolvable problems that you'll be grappling with for the next ten, twenty or fifty years." For us, that sixty-nine per cent statistic may as well have been ninety-six. We met late in life with values and habits already deeply set, with cultural and gender differences to boot.

In 2013, after a succession of conflicts in the previous year, we decided to give space to each other and Bill left me in Seattle with my daughter after New Year's Day to help his son in Boise. It was going to be our longest separation in four and a half years of marriage. We had been apart for only a couple of days here and there before that. Since Bill and I married and started cruising in an RV, we had been together 24/7, seven days a week.

We had actually been seeing a pastoral counselor, and before Bill left, we were directed to consider it a retreat, reflecting every single day we were apart, find meaning in a specific adventure in our four years of cruising, and recall how it really was with the other. Our counselor also asked us to read the book *Perfect Love, Imperfect Relationships*.

The first days without Bill were hard. Compounding the situation was the change in medications his doctor gave me for my increasing anxieties and my continuing breakouts of hives, acid reflux and heartburn. But fortunately in my life, I have survived and in fact prospered because of how I face problems. Those are times when I turn my attention to other aspects of my life. Soon, with all the free time I had, after my daughter and her family left for work or school, I reflected greatly and then focused my energies on compiling all my blog posts into one manuscript. I felt there was a bigger story to be told. That draft became the foundation of my first book.

When Bill came back on Valentine's Day, we realized that what we needed was a new phase of traveling. After having visited all the forty-nine American states on the continent, with nine Canadian provinces and six Mexican states in addition, we needed to move on to a discovery of the world. Also, we needed a better base from which to go on trips outside North America. We looked for one and, in October of the same year, we settled on Viewpoint in Mesa, Arizona. To date, I have been to forty-eight countries; Bill was with me in twenty-nine of those. Our base was no longer a parked RV; it had become an actual home, and it was a good place to be renewed between trips.

My great luck is that Bill is a man with a high emotional quotient (EQ). He has a twenty-nine-year marriage in his past life that ended only because his wife passed on due to cancer. My first marriage, to the father of my children, ended after nine years with a separation first and an annulment later. Even Bill's second marriage lasted eight years; mine only two. His constant request was for me to view the totality of the relationship and its long-term nature, not any specific situation and certainly not just the moment. In hindsight, he showed me how the firm commitment to stay together, despite differences, is one of the secrets to a lasting marriage.

Whereas my instinct was for fight and flight, I learned to calm down and later to compromise. I realized that there was no need to withdraw completely every time one encounters a difficulty, because staying offered much bigger rewards. It is no accident that the deep respect for being the persons we each were was behind the realization. We came to accept that we would never have been the least bit attracted to each other at the height of our careers. But at the age when we met, each of our pasts was the source of a deep respect for the other. I didn't have to lose my identity to be a wife. Neither did he, to be a husband. This is the second secret to a good marriage.

Finally, we had one thing that we solidly shared. We had both dreamed of the same thing when we retired from our stressful business lives. We share a deep passion to go and discover the world. So we extended our honeymoon for as long as we could. Every scenic sight became not just a marvel but also, at times, a coping mechanism. We both love to plan trips, enjoy each new place or experience, and relish looking back. Travel nurtured both of us and gave our life together the spices it needed to fuse the disparate flavors. This is secret number three.

Travels do not have to be just about physically going from one place to the next. They can also lead one to significant inner journeys. For me, one of those has unmistakably been to finally become a wife. My friends back in the Philippines still cannot believe it but they are happy for me. They admire Bill for knowing how to love their once famously difficult-to-handle friend. So I include here the following story about two of Bill's three visits to the Philippines and how he came to appreciate my friends, the Filipinos, and my homeland. It is my second most-widely-read blog post.

RELIVING WWII IN THE PHILIPPINES

At the end of the Spanish-American War in 1898, Spain ceded the Philippines to the US. Because of the strategic location of the islands, the US then built three major military bases in the country: Subic Naval Base in Zambales, Clark Air Force Base in Pampanga, and Fort Mills on Corregidor Island. And in 1941 the country became a major battlefront in the Pacific during WWII.

For a Filipino-American couple like Bill and me, this piece of history takes on a significance of more than double proportions. During Bill's first visit to the Philippines early in 2009 after our wedding, I took him to Subic and Clark; on the second visit in 2011, I took him to Corregidor. During both times, we relived WWII campaigns together in my home country.

Subic Base was a major ship-repair, supply, and rest and recreation facility of the US Navy. It was the largest overseas military installation of the United States Armed Forces after Clark Air Base.

Since the turnover of both to the Philippine government in 1991, however, Subic had become an industrial park, a tourist resort, and a residential haven.

One of my friends and her American husband live in a former officer's home with a very affordable long-term lease. She worked for the Subic Bay Development Corporation which was managing the reconstituted area. The tourist duty-free shops were still operating with many a bargain, the beaches still looked very inviting, and the hills still offered good jungle trips. Regularly, planeloads of Asians were being brought to its casinos for a gambling weekend.

When Bill and I scheduled a trip to Hong Kong, we chose a flight that departed from the Clark International Airport that had been built on the former Clark Air Base. It was a great alternative to the Ninoy Aquino International Airport (NAIA) in Metro Manila. The bus trip to and from Manila was one and a half-hour long, just as long as the trip to NAIA from many points in the city because of the typical horrendous traffic.

Clark has had a rebirth, especially because of its extensive facilities and land—14.3 square miles, with a military reservation extending north for another 230 square miles. The base was a stronghold of the combined Filipino and American forces and was a backbone of logistical support during the Vietnam War. In fact, it was there that Bill was able to fly a plane with a trainer from a Clark flying school.

While waiting for our flight we explored some of the areas around the airport. We discovered a lonely Goddess of Peace memorial donated by Japan and the previously mothballed Expo Center. Since this trip, I understand that the Clark Freeport Zone has grown. But it was our tour of the Villages—home of the native

Aetas in the surrounding hills—that became the highlight of our tour. We witnessed a wedding ritual, including the butchering of a cow for the feast.

Coming back from Hong Kong, we stayed in Clark for the night, and the next morning my girlfriends picked us up. After the famous pizzaninis at a restaurant called C!, we took the SCTEX, the new interchange connecting Subic and Clark, and proceeded to Montemar Beach Resort in Mariveles, Bataan, where one of them was a member.

From there, we were all able to retrace the steps of the sixty-mile Death March, which in 1942 resulted in very high fatalities inflicted among prisoners and civilians alike. After the Japanese bombed Pearl Harbor on Dec. 7, 1941, Bataan fell just four months later. 75,000 Filipino-American soldiers were forcibly transferred to the POW camp in Capas, Tarlac on the infamous march later judged by an Allied military commission to have been a Japanese war crime.

The March started in Mariveles near Montemar and markers are regularly placed on the road all along the route. On the way there, we all paid tribute to those who suffered during the tragic march at the huge cross on top of Mt. Samat. We also passed by Acuzar, the town right before Mariveles, to be inspired by lovely Las Casas Filipinas (Philippine Houses) by the sea, a neat cluster of restored ancestral Filipino homes purchased and painstakingly re-established there piece by piece from all over the Philippines.

On his second trip to the Philippines, Bill had a chance to see Corregidor Island, which lies at the mouth of Manila Bay. It is what the Americans called the "impregnable fortress." The island played a significant role in WWII both during the invasion and the subsequent liberation of the Philippines from Japanese forces. The hydrofoil trip to the island took just one and a half hours from the Folk Arts Theatre built on reclaimed land on Manila Bay.

Colorful tramvias, replicas of the old trollies, took us around the island. But we immediately saw evidence of the gruesome battle that lasted five months. There was the skeleton of heavily bombed Mile-long Barracks—the longest single military barracks in the world which housed 8,000 soldiers—and the remains of the cross-shaped hospital which the Japanese destroyed despite war treaties.

There were also many fitting tributes to those who bravely defended the island—the Pacific War Memorial with its altar and Eternal Flame, the Filipino Heroes Memorial with fourteen murals of Philippine history, and a statue of Gen. Douglas Macarthur, where he declared," I shall return," as he escaped to Australia. The island fell to the Japanese on May 6, 1942, not even a month after the Fall of Bataan. Three years after, the island was retaken.

The Malinta Tunnel Night Tour gave us the most descriptive retelling of the life of soldiers on the island fortress. The tunnel is a two-and-a-half mile network of laterals on Malinta (full of leeches) Hill. At times bending low to pass through narrower sub-laterals, we experienced utter darkness, felt whiffs of cooler air from the vent passages, and visited the 1,000-bed hospital that replaced the hospital that had been completely destroyed outside. We even retraced the escape route of Gen. MacArthur and visited the well-preserved space reserved for President Manuel Quezon, the petroleum storage facilities, the soldiers' quarters, and bizarrely a Japanese soldier's femur.

Taking these two trips with Bill made them doubly significant for me. First, it was as if I was presenting my husband to my father who fought with Americans and my mother who learned the Japanese language to interpret for Filipino and American soldiers. The trips were made during the first three crucial years of our marriage, and the first two of our RVing years. They gave Bill an early appreciation of the closeness of Filipino-American relations. The trips became quite symbolic for us and our early struggles as a couple.

2

MORE THAN A WRITER

§

How many times have we heard or even said the maxim, "It's not the destination; it's the journey"? I agree wholeheartedly. But, you know, I say that it's even more than the just the journey. Eventually what will matter most is the story. When the traipsing traveler becomes the spirited storyteller, then the experience can be relived many more times.

Retelling the story can be by speaking, uttering the words with the accompanying non-verbal expressions for emphasis. That's easy. In fact, during my Toastmaster days, I delighted in doing this with flair, coaching others to do the same and help them win championships. But now, I prefer to "put words on paper, giving flight to thoughts that tongue cannot set free," as a former suitor once wrote me. After my retirement, besides becoming a wife, I have also become a writer. The road to becoming one was accidental. And it has also not been easy.

First of all, my brain is largely unbalanced. It leans heavily to the left. From a BS degree in Mathematics and a career in IT and the business world, it was hard trying to awaken the creative right half of my brain. I had been used to writing proofs of theorems and hypotheses first, and then business project proposals and board reports later. Theses and dissertations in my master's and doctoral programs did not help.

Besides, English is not my native tongue. I was born in the slums of Manila. I got a great education through the Philippine public elementary school system, a high school scholarship to the American School (now called the International School of Manila) and a science scholarship at the University of the Philippines. English may have been the medium of instruction at all these levels. Still, Tagalog has a very different syntax. Thinking in Tagalog is quite "foreign," and that's how I still think.

Bill edits my rough drafts until today: he used to return pages of my early writings almost completely red from all his markings; but I soldiered on. The travel blog, besides being the best way to remember our RVing adventures, became a great way to practice. As we were constantly traveling, I was constantly writing. By 2013, I had written almost 300 blog posts. A fellow camper told me about EntreCard, a group of bloggers who supported and read each other's work. A couple of hundred started to read my posts while I read theirs in return.

When social media exploded, a few of my posts went viral, some getting 10,000, 20,000, 30,000 views (those are reprinted in this book). I was inspired. Visits to authors' homes, museums or tombs—among them Edgar Allan Poe, Ernest Hemingway, Henry Wadsworth Longfellow, and Robert Frost—lifted my writing spirits even more. It was on my unexpected trip to the Authors' Ridge in Concord, Massachusetts where four literary greats are buried—Ralph Waldo Emerson, Henry David Thoreau, Nathaniel

Hawthorne, and Louisa May-Alcott—when I concluded that writing was what I wanted to do.

I have already told you about the significance of our separation for more than a month beginning after New Year's Day in 2013. When Bill came back, he was so happy to have had a meaningful month and a half with his son; and I felt blessed to have had productive time, coming up with the draft of my first book. In the next two years, that first draft was edited, polished, and self-published into *Carolina: Cruising*, the book tour for which started in June of 2015.

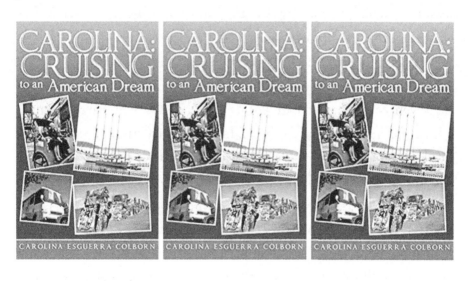

Thankfully, over time, my writing improved. After all, I have been writing for almost ten years now. But I still do not have the flair for idiomatic, local American English—that which is spoken in the streets, in homes, in the gathering places of America. That is why I have the TV on the whole day, so I can imbibe more by hearing while I am on my computer. Unfortunately, it drives Bill crazy, and he retreats to his man-cave. Actually, I do have an office. I just don't use it, and prefer to stay in the more expansive living room. So, we are now adding an Arizona room overlooking the small patio/ garden that I could use. But that is perhaps too much information.

Writing travel journals was a practical start. I didn't want to forget what I felt, saw, and experienced in places I had only seen in pictures before. But, just like other writers, I wanted to express more of my innermost feelings and thoughts, even if it made me vulnerable. I wanted to connect more. There is so much I want to share, and my time here is becoming ever shorter. It is good that the weeks we spend on the road have lately become fewer, giving me more time to wonder about our wanderings and to put on paper the lessons learned, the changes made, and the insights gained so that they might be of help to others, too.

In other words, I now also write about the other not-so-obvious journeys, the inner ones. Since shifting gears when I approached the big seven-zero, I have created more travel essays than travel journals. I love them; and they led me right in the direction of this second book in which I have compiled, polished, threaded and expanded the best-loved and most widely-read of them.

And, of course, I am now also into freelance writing. I have written off and on for three online publications before; but now I am a regular paid expert/contributor to *TravelAwaits*, an online travel magazine for those over fifty, with about two original unpublished articles a month. Six of them are reprinted here. We won't get rich by it, but I certainly like that my work is regularly published in a well-regarded online travel magazine.

Later, I will probably undertake a last phase of traveling, and will have even more inner journeys to tell. By that time, I can picture Bill and me, smiling, holding hands, whiling our hours away in our rocking chairs, even looking at past blog posts and photo albums. If we are lucky, I may still be writing new pages, and he will still be editing them.

TAKING AN INTEREST IN PHOTOGRAPHY

Bill had the foresight to invest in a Nikon DSLR as part of our essential travel gear right from the start. Thus, photos began to populate my blog posts (plus Facebook and Twitter and now Pinterest). As some photographer once said, "Once you learn to care, you can record images in your mind and film. There is no difference." So this was another way travel changed me. I was given the best motivation to capture great moments in pictures (and now, in videos). *Carolina: Cruising* was published with some fifty photos, and this book has around the same number.

When we began to slow down and settled in Viewpoint, part of its appeal was some fifty clubs. One of them, the Viewpoint Photography Club, became my favorite. Fortunately, senior members took time to mentor me. I look at my earlier attempts, and regret how I was not able to capture those scenes well. Sadly, those scenes are as good as lost forever unless we go back. Thankfully, for our later travels, I now have examples of photos that tell great stories.

I took one of blue doors that led to our room at the bed and breakfast where we stayed in Tunisia. That photo won Best of Show, People's Choice and Judges' Choice Awards in the first Photo Show I ever entered; but that photo could very well never have seen the light of day. We almost did not go to Tunisia. A month before our trip, a massacre of tourists had just been orchestrated by terrorists in Tunis, the capital.

I was immediately bumped to the next category, from Bronze to Silver, but even if competition had become stiffer, in the following year I still won first place in two categories, Black & White (The Salisbury Cathedral Close) and Street Photography (The Brighton UK Wheel). Seeing that my passion had grown, on my seventieth birthday Bill gifted me with a Sony mirrorless digital camera to replace the bulky Nikon DSLR. It has the power of a DSLR, but it is as compact as a point and shoot. Recently, my children have even gifted me with an expensive camera drone.

In 2018 I had a quite a heyday. The process of selecting what to enter was tricky and hard. Bill and three more advanced photographers helped me choose the best ten of them to enter at that year's Photo Show. I made my first dollars from my photography, and each of the photos I submitted won in their categories, six of them first place. I was bumped to Gold.

Sadly, I am no longer able to enter the Photo Shows because, beginning in 2019, we made Mexico our third home, where we spend every January to March while it is cold in Phoenix. But I consoled myself with the thought that I really do not want to become a professional photographer; I just want to be a story teller whose photos can help relive our adventures better than just my words can ever do.

Today, our new pace of travel gives me more time to improve my photo-taking skills. As I polish my travel essays, I hope my photos will also tell better tales. In the march of time, as the photographer Ansell Adams once said: "When words become unclear, I shall focus with photographs. When images become inadequate, I shall be content with silence." That may be nearly impossible, according to Bill; but these words of wisdom will keep me grounded. I can see the time when my words and photos will keep me traveling; even if only through the landscapes of my mind.

3

A BETTER WANDERER

§

M y husband and I have traveled together from the time we
met in July 2007; that is some thirteen years. We began as
tourists, traveling for pleasure, visiting places out of curiosity. Take
our trip to the Arctic Circle in Canada's Yukon as an example. We
wanted the bragging rights, so we braved three days and two nights
on a dirt-gravel road just to set foot inside it and get a photograph of
us under the marker of that special spot.

An RV gave us the means to move around North America in a
relentless and incisive fashion. In the first eight months, we would
stay three to four days at a place. Later, our stays became two to
three weeks at a time. Then we would winter in Arizona for four
months a year. That was when we began to venture out of North
America. I really cannot say when we started to be more than tourists; what I know is that I have even become an accidental pilgrim in
the vignette I have added to this chapter.

An Explorer is defined as a person who combs an area for
the purpose of discovery. When we became members of a

nationwide network of campgrounds and bought the 37.5-foot Class A motorhome, we invested big in the RV cruising lifestyle. Staying longer in a place, we were able to explore an area more completely using the dinghy we towed, a Saturn compact sedan. Bill and I researched the place and scheduled daily explorations. We followed the "three-hour rule," or three hours of driving one-way to allow for at least six hours at a destination in a twelve-hour day.

In Ontario, Canada, for example, we saw the city's four faces—a government hub in Ottawa, a bustling metropolitan center in Toronto, a famous tourist destination in Niagara, and the rural town where we were camped. But a more recent example is our exploration of three countries from our base in the small town of Oberstaufen in Germany. We were there for only a week, but the trains took us to St. Gallen, Switzerland, Vaduz, Lichtenstein, and Uberlinger, Germany.

An Adventurer, on the other hand, is a person who has or seeks activities in places for excitement or an unusual experience, despite the risks they may entail. I must admit that Bill is more of the adventurer between the two of us. He scuba dives, skis, flies a plane, etc. I just play with my smartphone or laptop, an armchair sort of girl. I love watching tennis, but I can't play it. I have been, and probably will always be a nerd.

For example, when we once spent a summer RVing in Alaska and we stumbled upon the Worthington Glacier on the road to Valdez, Bill immediately went up to climb it while I stayed behind. I was scared I might hurt myself or be frozen stiff. When we went with Bill's high school friends for a reunion in Crested Butte, Colorado, everyone went river-rafting. I stayed behind to imagine the fun times they must be having and write a blog post about it. At Grandfather's Mountain in North Carolina, while driving the Blue

Ridge Parkway, Bill bravely went across the Mile-High Swinging Bridge. I gladly stayed behind to take his photo.

But now I can proudly say I have conquered not one but two glaciers. In fact, I was even able to ride a helicopter in Kauai, Hawaii to see places unreachable by car. Furthermore, I have gone down to the bottom of the ocean in a submarine. Come to think of it, not many people can say they have gone RVing. Indeed, that was basically a big adventure in itself.

A third kind of a special traveler is a pilgrim. This is a person who journeys, especially over a long distance, to some sacred place as an act of devotion, or even as an original settler. Being both Catholics, it was easy for Bill and me to be pilgrims together. In fact, it made our life together more easily and more deeply connected.

Once we diverted from our planned itinerary north to Minnesota, turning west to visit the Grotto of the Redemption in

West Bend, Iowa. There we saw the complex of nine grottos made from forty-three different kinds of donated gems, built entirely by the hands of two men, a priest and an assistant (and then continued by another priest when the first passed on).

Clearly, we have crossed the line from being tourists to becoming explorers. Although I will not often be the adventurer that Bill is, I will nevertheless claim some success in this area. But the kind of traveler I hope to be more of is that of a pilgrim. Deepening our faith will come naturally and be more significant when we shift gears once again for our last traveling days.

ACCIDENTAL PILGRIMS

Sometimes we visit a place because we long to see it; sometimes we go because of a whim. I went to the Balkans for a purely practical purpose. This cheapskate, yours truly, found a promo that offered a week at the Balkan Jewel Resort for unbelievably few timeshare points. There were pros and cons. October 2015 would still be cold for a woman from the tropics. And the Balkan countries are among the least visited in Europe.

Bill did not want to go but Jingjing, the PR strategist who helped launch my first book in the Philippines, was waiting to take me up on my promise of a break together. It was going to add to her goal of sixty-five countries by the time she turned sixty-five in two years. At sixty-seven, I needed catching up fast, too. And it would be off the beaten path, curiosity at a low price.

She arrived in Sofia, Bulgaria from Manila an hour earlier than I did and found the hotel driver who had a sign bearing my name. Her trademark smile warmly greeted my arrival from Phoenix. Midway in the two-hour drive to Razlog, we asked to stop for food. Our driver fidgeted, "No English." Luckily, out of nowhere, McDonalds' arches appeared like a double rainbow with a pot of burgers more precious than gold.

When we arrived at the Balkan Jewel Resort, we were pleasantly surprised that our studio was more like a one bedroom suite. But it was the next morning when views from our windows completely blew us away. They were of the postcard-pretty Pirin Mountains bathed in the splendor of fall. Jovial locals boisterously babbling led us to the bountiful brunch buffet. Then we splashed into the indoor pool, and tried the exotic ceramic spa lounge chairs.

Razlog is a ski resort area and Bansko, only seven minutes away, is a cultural center. The duo is the Bulgarians' winter destination of choice. A shuttle brought us to downtown Bansko. The only traffic we encountered was a large herd of cute sheep with rotund butts. With just our animated gestures and without words, our driver brought us to the town's pride, the Holy Trinity Church.

The Eastern Orthodox Church looked small from the out-side. We found out that they intentionally built it sunken below the ground to deflect Turkish imperialist ambition. When we got inside, the smell of centuries-old white fir was distinctive. The wooden-framed church was a masterpiece, richly colored and decorated like no church I have ever seen before. It looked more like a festive Eastern Opera House just before its grand opening. There were brilliant frescoes, twelve radiant pillars—one for each Apostle—and a floor-to-ceiling and wall-to-wall altar-piece of glittering icons.

I didn't expect Jingjing's reaction: "I wonder where we can find a Catholic church?" In a week of rest, she yearned for a familiar place of worship. Alas, it would not be in nearby Sofia, the modern capital of Bulgaria, or Plovdiv, her ancient city. We searched the Web that night and found that Mother Teresa, who would soon be beatified a saint—she was, eleven months later—was an Albanian. She was born in Skopje, Macedonia when it was still part of Yugoslavia, three and a half hours away. Always up for an adventure, Jingjing cried, *"Taralets!"* (Tagalog colloquialism for "Let's go!")

The Resort arranged an inexpensive taxi ride for us. Alas, our driver spoke no English, so we were left with the preoccupation of admiring Bulgarian hillsides turning into huge canvasses of fall colors. As we approached Macedonia the countryside became greener, even if the black poplars, standing tall and elegant in rows, had shed almost all their leaves. Our driver breezed through the border. Balkan languages seemed to have a lot in common.

When we checked in at Ibis Skopje, we were happy to find that everyone spoke English. When they found out we were there for Mother Teresa, the receptionist asked, "Are you interested in a small church another one and a half hours away in Letnica, Kosovo?" Also previously part of Yugoslavia, it was where Mother Teresa's mother took her when she was just seventeen; and there she heard her calling to serve the poorest of the poor. My friend was like a kid just told she was going to Disney. Of course, there was another excited *"Taralets!"* Good thing the additional taxi ride was also inexpensive.

We had an hour to visit the Mother Teresa Memorial House a few blocks away. They built it on the grounds of the church of her baptism, the day she recognized as her birthday. At the Chapel her photo was at the center of floor-to-ceiling, wall-to-wall glass windows laced with intricate ironworks. Natural light streamed through, enveloping us in delicate shadows. We were in awe, and silent prayer became our only conversation. At the House we posed by her childhood bed and imagined her veined, wrinkled hand writing those loving letters from Calcutta. Her life was an enormous contribution the Balkans gave to the world.

Back at the hotel a muscular middle-aged man was waiting for us. We were dumbfounded when he asked, "May I ask why you want to go to Letnica?" Our new driver spoke incredibly good English but also deftly handled the strict scrutiny at the border checkpoint. Kosovo remains a disputed territory even after her declaration of independence from Serbia in 2008 when Yugoslavia was dissolved. He told us the horrific story as we made our way through war-torn villages: "Look at what the war did. There's another skeleton of a house. See those writings on the walls." The Kosovo War left over ten thousand dead and over a million displaced.

Then he slowed down to show us a large embankment perpendicular to the road, painted with a map of the area. "Kosovo is Little Albania; ninety percent Albanian," he said. "But they are Kosovar Albanians. They want to be a separate country." With a Muslim majority, there were many mosques. But it was the identical houses, in pairs, trios, even fives, that caught our interest. "It is a tradition of regular familial reunions. Brothers live side by side, in identical looking homes," he explained.

In no time we reached Letnica, a semi-deserted hamlet of a handful of households. Every August it comes alive as thousands of people, including Croats returning to homes they had abandoned, come to celebrate the Feast of the Black Madonna. Inside the simple white church sitting atop a hill, Mother Teresa's unadorned photo hangs near the uncomplicated altar. Then we got goose bumps when we thought we saw her ghost as an old woman, wrinkled and bent like we remembered her, hobbled into the church.

By nightfall, as we were we were approaching Skopje, a cross shining brightly high up in the evening sky caused us to look at each other, transfixed and entranced. Our driver noticed this and excitedly drove us to a place from where we could take better pictures. But my Nikon just couldn't capture the magic. "It's the 217-foot tall Millennium Cross," he said proudly, "built on top of Vodno Mountain to celebrate 2,000 years of Christianity. It is the sign that unites all our faiths." He was right. Catholic, Orthodox or Protestant, Christianity is ideally one and the same.

Over an authentic Macedonian dinner, a fusion of Turkish and Greek flavors, our driver suggested we continue to Nis, Serbia. "It would probably add just five hours to your trip back to Razlog, but that's where Constantine the Great, the first Christian Roman emperor, was born," he said. We followed his suggestion, but because borders between Kosovo and Serbia remain closed, our route had us going east and north of Skopje.

We learned that Constantine's father was a Roman Emperor who had to marry another woman to legitimize his rule. Helena, his mother, was a consort sent away to Nis. But by the time his father died, Constantine had become a legendary warrior and was acclaimed Emperor. His conversion to Christianity was historic. History credits Helena with the guidance that led to Constantine's great reign. For this and her acts of piety and kindness, all of Christendom later also revered her as a saint, just like her son. It was providential for Jingjing to come all this way; her real name is Elena, a derivative of Helena. She is a single parent who raised not just one son, but three and a daughter. At the newly built Church of Constantine and Helena in Nis, she finally found a comfortable place of worship.

All the way back to Razlog, we saw more glistening crosses of various sizes atop the hills. By week's end, we realized we had experienced more than we had ever expected. Jingjing added four new countries to her list. I loved Balkan culture, religion, and affordability. And we met drivers we will never forget. But our final takeaway was more precious than all these. The Balkans gave new meaning to the cliché "It's not about the destination; it's the journey." Our trip turned into a search for something sacred and deeply personal. We became more than tourists in the Balkans. We were accidental pilgrims.

4

FINALLY, A MOTHER

§

As a jet-setting executive in Manila, I was away from home most of the time, and it sure cost me a lot. I ended up a single parent, and had to stay away even more, leaving my three young daughters to the care of nannies, cooks, and drivers. In my retired life in America, I had hoped for the chance to make up for all that absence. It would have been much easier if we were all together in one place. But, as luck would have it—or as a consequence of the life I lived—we are all far apart from each other. My eldest, Trisha, lives in San Francisco (Seattle before that), my middle daughter, Claudine, has been in Calgary ever since she left Manila, and my youngest, April, makes Melbourne (London before that) home. This is also a major reason we travel a lot.

In the following three vignettes from my blog posts, I give you a glimpse of my second chance at motherhood. The first tells how I meddled in the wedding of April in Scotland. Mothers are absolutely not supposed to do that. Unfortunately, mothers-of-the-bride, usually do. So how could I ever expect to be viewed in a better light? In Canada, when my middle daughter Claudine sent me a plane ticket to come help her take care of her three sons, Bill and I left no stone unturned to complete our exploration of the Canadian Rockies every weekend. One of those coincided with Mother's Day, and I was again touched by what my daughters thought best to give me. I wondered why they always do. In the last vignette, I finally found out why.

MEDDLING IN THE UK

April felt abandoned when I left Manila to retire and find a new life in America. Although she had already been working for two years, she still felt that way, perhaps because I had treated her as cherished above all, the way a *Bunso* (youngest child) is usually treated. She quickly applied for admission to American universities to pursue her MBA.

April had graduated *magna cum laude* from the University of the Philippines, so I knew that would be a breeze. Besides, her career at Andersen Consulting, an American IT consulting firm, had been stellar. But we discovered that there was a different obstacle. She was denied a student visa because the Commission on Immigration Services felt she would be entirely dependent on me and Bill. Again, I felt like a huge failure.

She finally took matters into her own hands and transferred to another global IT company, which soon assigned her to a major project in the UK. She fell in love with the country. When her Filipino boyfriend Clint felt that she might not go back to the Philippines, her life turned into a fairy tale. He followed her; and they were wed at the lovely fifteenth century Guthrie Castle in Forfar, Scotland.

For two days, the two families and the couple's friends were hosted within its twenty-two charming bedrooms and treated to a private exclusive tour of the Scottish Highlands the day after. Of course, I strongly suggested my friends as godparents, tried to influence her choice of the bridal gown, and encouraged the use of kilts for men and fascinators for women at the party. Then, horror of horrors, I delivered a long mother-of-the-bride speech.

I meddled such that, after the wedding, Bill and I went with them to their darling two-bedroom townhome in Newcastle-upon-Tyne in England. Our bedroom overlooked a wall with interesting graffiti beyond their backyard's vine of purple and white flowers. I was so glad the room also had an elliptical machine that helped me shed some of the pounds I had gained during our cruise and road trips through Scandinavia, Iceland, and the UK that preceded the wedding.

While they went for a short honeymoon in London, Bill and I toured Newcastle, the bustling capital of northeastern England. We visited the Hadrian Wall, the legendary Roman legacy in the UK, and the nearby city of Durham. But soon Bill had to leave, the couple came back, and Clint's meddling mother-in-law stayed behind.

They both worked so most of the time I was left alone in the apartment. I made it a point to have a great dinner waiting for them after work. Every weekend, they took me on a tour. First was to the nearby small town of Corbridge to show me how they enjoy sipping wine at the small English village's town circle. Tynemouth in the outskirts of Newcastle was a revelation, too. The fishing town of Whitby had a lot to offer: the famous Abbey, its cemetery, the outdoor Shakespeare play on one hill, the Captain Cook monument on another hill across the waters, and the port in the center with great fish and chips to eat and crabs to take home. Finally, I witnessed reenactments of medieval life, another Abbey in ruins, and the monastery's wine-making prowess on the Holy Island of Lindisfarne, connected to the mainland during low tide.

One afternoon April and Clint also took me to an outdoor play near their offices. I had not been to one in such a long time so, despite being windy, it was so much fun. Another time, we went to a Western Cowboys and Cowgirls birthday party for the little boy of one of their couple-friends where the *piece de resistance* was the traditional lechon (whole roasted pig). Oh how I have missed this Filipino delicacy. The Newcastle Filipino community, especially those from the CFC (Christians for Christ) households they were a part of, sure knew how to celebrate events and keep the Filipino spirit in UK burning brightly.

As a matter of fact, one time they coaxed me into joining an outing and give the brand new couple a break from the meddling. We went to the High Force Waterfalls on the River Tees, near Middleton-in-Teesdale, Teesdale County in Durham. The waterfall is within the North Pennines Area of Outstanding Natural Beauty (AONB). Despite popular belief that it is the highest waterfall in England, at seventy-one feet, Cautley Spout, in Cumbria's Howgill Fells, is almost 650 feet high. But it is a cascade, while High Force is a plunge fall. Since we all still had time to spare before the afternoon sun turned into an evening glow, we stopped by to do some strawberry picking at a farm. You cannot imagine my joy at seeing such HUGE strawberries growing straight out of the earth-clinging vines. We ate as many fresh strawberries as our stomachs could bear and brought home a full basket for the couple.

Yes, I meddled in my daughter's new married life in the UK. Judging by their cozy home, the fun-loving and spiritual people they chose as friends, and the awesome sightseeing all around, they were blessed to start with such a charmed happy life. I had hoped it would continue long and well through the arrival of babies. At the end of four years, however, the fairy tale bubble burst. My daughter found out she could not convert her visa to that of an immigrant because of an original technicality. At least, this one wasn't my fault.

A MOTHER'S DAY GETAWAY

In 2016, my middle daughter Claudine in Canada was being given more and more responsibilities in her company. Her job had become more demanding; and she was on the road to becoming a Director. She sent me a ticket to come help her take care of Enzo, Kai, and Jax ages eleven, four, and two at the time. Bill followed after two weeks.

Luckily, the four Canadian national parks in the Rockies are just an hour and a half, to three hours and a half, away from her home. In four weekends, therefore, Bill and I left no stone unturned at these contiguous parks that together comprise a UNESCO World Heritage Site. We had visited the more popular Banff and Jasper National Parks in 2009 when I was taking care of my first grandson, Enzo. On the first two weekends we went to see the other two less known national parks, Kootenay and Yoho.

The third weekend included the second Sunday of May, when much of the world toasts mothers. My three daughters have kept the tradition of giving me gifts, and when Bill and I became full-time travelers, they changed them from jewelry, apparel, or accessories to experiences like fine dining, tours, and cruises. This year, it was a weekend getaway at the Fairmont Banff Springs Hotel.

The historic, large castle-like building, for which the hotel chain is noted, was built in 1888 from the era of railway tourism. Today, it is a Banff emblem, set off on its own in a wooded area, appearing like a dream as we drove up the road on the hill. Our well-appointed room at the floor just below the top looked out to the lovely view of the Bow River tumbling over a cliff-like rise.

Bill did not want to be outdone and took care of all the memorable meals. He drove me to Lake Louise, that postcard-pretty place about thirty minutes from Banff. I had been there twice before, the first time without Bill. On my second visit, it was the height of summer and the glacier sliding down into the lake looked much thinner. This time it was spring, and it was in its full glory. We could not canoe around the lake however, unlike the previous visit, because the ice was just starting to thaw. But the sight was certainly more impressive. After many photos we took from many angles, Bill led me to the Fairmont Chateau Lake Louise (of the same chain as our Banff hotel) with a commanding view of the lovely sight. He had reserved a table with a huge picture window looking out on the perfect scene for a pre-Mother's Day lunch.

After lunch, we proceeded to our premium hotel for the night. The staff told us to check out the pool area. We found an Olympic-sized pool that had a secluded large hot tub at one end and elegant chaise lounge chairs all around. It was a pleasant surprise to find out that the staff was actually referring to the pool outdoors, where everyone was having the time of their lives. Heated, and with magnificent views of the Bow Valley Mountains, I could have stayed there forever, but Bill pulled me away. He had reservations for my pre-Mother's Day dinner at the Rundle Lounge.

The next morning we just walked around the town of Banff, simply savoring the crispness and coolness of the air, bathed by the brightness of the sun. There is special magic in shopping and strolling among stores and streets surrounded by towering mountains. Then Bill took me to a Mother's Day brunch at an Irish Pub where he had his much-missed shepherd's pie, while I had my first taste of Yorkshire pudding with bits of delicious roast beef inside.

After a room service breakfast, we checked out from Fairmont Banff Springs Hotel and moved to Holiday Inn in Canmore, the town near the southeast boundary of the Banff National Park. Since the city was chosen to host the Nordic events of the 1988 Winter Olympics, tourism has flourished and the town population is now over 12,000, surpassing Banff's 9,000.

We had not been there before, so we shopped and strolled at a more leisurely pace. It has the small town feel but the same magic from the ever-present snow-capped mountains all around. At a small park on a river bank, a concrete sculpture of a humongous head half-buried in the ground captured my fancy and was a spot for a lot of photos. The Canmore Hotel sat on the main street, as it has for over 100 years, making it one of the most distinct landmarks in the city. I was also fascinated by an odd garden that continuously produced soap bubbles from a hidden machine.

Then Bill took me to a huge Mother's Day late lunch and early dinner at Santa Lucia Trattoria, a small Italian restaurant that seats only about forty people. The next morning, before checking out, we had a post-Mother's Day breakfast at the famous Rocky Mountain Bagel Company downtown that featured dozens of delectable bagel varieties. And then we met Claudine, her husband Arnold, and all the grandsons at a huge Western buffet for a festive post-Mother's Day Lunch.

My daughters and Bill outdid themselves this year. It was not only another great break from babysitting but a Mother's Day Getaway I will forever treasure. It always made me wonder why they don't toast me on Father's Day instead. After all, I was an absentee-mother, too busy at my career and preferring the role of a provider.

I hoped it was not only because they felt an obligation to make me feel appreciated, especially on Mother's Day. Bill ended my musings with, "Look at what I do for you. You are not even my mother."

IN MY DAUGHTER'S EYES

On my last weekend in Canada, it was already late spring so the weather was forecast to be good. The sun should have been out. But, true only to itself, the weather took a sudden, nasty turn. We still proceeded with our plan to go to the Glacier Skywalk and stayed in Banff for the night. We hoped it would clear the following day, but it didn't. The operator at the Columbia Icefields Visitor Center was encouraging, saying, "It's snowing, but it's gorgeous out here." I have suffered through many Philippine storms, but snow takes me directly inside a freezer. However, Bill declared, "It's now or never!" We had to go. It was our last chance.

In 2009 we had passed through the Icefields Parkway, one of National Geographic's "twenty drives of a lifetime." We were then driving our first motor home, hurrying to reach Jasper for a week of "glamping" or glamorous camping, a current trend. It was the height of summer then, but this time it was still spring so we were going to see a new perspective.

At more than 6,000 feet in elevation, the evergreens were still frosty. Snow was still settled on each branch. "You have to take my picture!" I insisted. After a few seconds of hesitation, I bravely stepped out into the cold. Wet fluffy things instantly brushed against my face. I shivered, but a different kind of warmth came over me as I "smelled" chestnuts roasting. It was wonderful to get a whiff of Christmas, and have my Christmas photo taken, in June.

There were already all kinds of RVs on the road: small camper vans, large motorhomes, and tagalongs like trailers and fifth-wheels.

I wished we had brought ours. I would always make sweet hot cocoa during chilly drives. Our 37.5-foot motorhome would have struck a bold stance against those glacier-draped mountains. She would have been part of parade of models showcasing the cruising lifestyle on the road. Sigh.

When we reached the Visitor Center, the snowfall got heavier. I certainly didn't need a red carpet, but having to negotiate a huge parking lot under those conditions was not the welcome we wanted. A beaming bright yellow loaded Hummer prominently displayed in front of the Center erased my blues. Bill chuckled when I asked, "How did they know my favorite color is yellow?" She was the star of the vehicles on ice that had been parading before us all morning. My day magically brightened. It was as if the sun had broken through.

Once I stepped inside the Center, warmth immediately enveloped me. I rushed to the tourist-filled Gift Shop, but Bill put an end to the shopping, wanting to go to the Cafeteria. I was reluctant at first but, once there, we were comforted by bowls of chicken noodle soup so good, steaming hot, and tasting homemade. Satisfied, we stepped into the Observation Deck for another whiff of the wintry world.

The Athabasca Glacier is the Icefield's biggest. But it appeared strangely smaller from the time we'd seen it in 2009. We wanted to know why, but it was time to board the shuttle. Besides, the snowfall was getting even heavier. It was the driver who answered our burning question, "The Glacier recedes about five meters a year. Our operations may cease in as early as fifteen years." What a hint of global warming. In a geologic sense, we had made it just in time.

I shouldn't have been glad. What waited for us at the Glacier Skywalk was a huge disappointment. Pictures of it in brochures were the exact opposite. It was all there, the largest cantilevered platform in America with an enormous, polygonal steel support shaped like an H, holding the all-glass curved tension bridge that loops about 150 degrees around the cliff's edge at a thousand feet high. The interpretive trail leading to it is about 400 meters long. Sadly, there was absolutely no hint of the glaciers. They were all hiding. I cried, "We have to get a refund. Bill merely shrugged, "Good luck!"

Used to making the best of bad situations, I turned my attention to my outfit. It had accidentally come together. The red beanie I'd just bought at the Gift Shop perfectly matched the red gloves my daughter lent me and the red scarf I had brought with me for the trip. The trio brightened the black winter jacket Claudine had given me to use, giving color to all the gloom and gray. It became apparent to me why I was at the Skywalk despite the snow, and why all day I had been seeing notions of models. I was going to have a fashion show of my own.

Custodians kept wiping off the snow from the slippery Skywalk, turning it into MY Catwalk. Bill stepped up to the role of a fashion photographer, taking my photos at many spots in different poses. Forgetting that Bill had taken off his gloves to fiddle with the Nikon settings and to set up the tripod, I snapped out of my trance only when he hollered, "My fingers are already frozen!" Even that didn't diminish the fun. I had actually gotten to like snow. With Bill's help, it had made me a glamorous model, at sixty-eight.

Back at my daughter's home, I was hugged tight by my grandkids. I couldn't stop showing them my photos straight off the camera. Claudine shook her head in disbelief and sighed, "Mama, you're much more than a fashion model!" I was taken aback. That's when I realized that being a jet-setting grand nanny is not about visiting new landmarks although that was a great perk. I found out why the notion of models stayed with me all day. In Calgary, I had the most liberating moment of my life. I found out that, in my daughter's eyes, I may not have been the best role model, but I was good enough. It did not matter that I hadn't had a lot of time with my children. What mattered more was that I had shown them enough good examples. One thing was also sure. They were smart enough to pick up the good and discard the bad. It was not really that I was an inadequate mother. It was just that I had always wished I could have given them more.

5

AND THEN A PROMOTION

§

It's the most wonderful thing that my daughters have even given me a precious third chance. They had promoted me to the best job in the whole wide world: a thrilled grandmother to seven special people. My two eldest granddaughters were born in Manila, so I only had oversight over their care when they were young and lived with us in our Makati condo. During my retirement in America, five more grandchildren have been born, all boys.

Now let me tell you how important it is that I babysit my grandsons. You see, up to the time the first one, Baby Enzo, was born in Calgary, Alberta, I had four sisters, three daughters, and two granddaughters. I so wanted to take care of a baby boy. I was living in Texas at the time and sadly, my second husband would not give me permission to go to Calgary to take care of my first ever grandson. He really did not appreciate Filipino traditions, nor understand my heart. That was the last straw. I filed for divorce and gave up smoking to earn the right to take care of Enzo. I immediately flew to Calgary.

The following are three vignettes to show how my new job grew over the years. The first is about my being a nanny in London for youngest daughter April's first child Kyrie during his first month of life. The second is not really about babysitting. I was just keeping Kenji, my nine-year old grandson, company during the big transition year of his family. And the last is about my twenty-three-year-old granddaughter taking it upon herself to take care of Bill and me in San Francisco. Together, the three show a full circle. It begins with my taking care of a grandchild when he is born and ends when a grandchild, in turn, takes care of us. It is why it is so joyful to reach this stage of life.

A NANNY IN LONDON

Kyrie was born at 7:40 pm on September 14, 2015 at the Queen Charlotte Hospital in London (April had asked for a move to London from Newcastle). He came by C-section after her heroic attempt of forty hours in labor and sixteen hours of being induced. No wonder, he was all of eight pounds six ounces; such a big baby boy for my five-foot-two 120-pound daughter.

Bill and I had just been in Kauai for two days when we got the news. Just a day after we got back to Phoenix after short trips to Maui and Oahu, I was on board a Norwegian Air flight to London. Clint was at the airport to pick me up. Soon my seventh grandchild was in my arms. I don't know if I just imagined it but I could have sworn he said, "Hi GrandMum!" in that cute British accent.

The couple had just had an exhausting two weeks. They had their hands full, and my daughter had a fever. The cute baby boy woke up every two hours to be nursed, burped, and changed. It was so good to be able to help, talk to, and play with him. But changing nappies—how I wished Bill had been there to help me, just as he did with Jax and Kai. But Clint, working from home, came to the rescue each time. I promise to improve on this skill with my great grandkids.

I delighted in my tasks that included making meals for our little family. Local grocer Sainsbury was just two floors below their two-bedroom flat. For special cuts of meat, the butcher was just a short block away. Across from him was the fruits and vegetable co-op. An artisan bread shop completed my needs two doors away. Even a wet market took only four bus stops and came complete with a Filipino store. I loved the local life in this part of London.

Just eight bus stops away was Westfield Mall, site of the 1906 Summer Olympics. The place used to be part of what was called White City because every edifice was white. That is where I met two of my friends for lunch: a colleague from the Institute of Advanced Computer Technology who had made London home; and a for-mer mentor at NCR Corporation Philippines who was also visiting London at the time. From the Mall, my mentor and I proceeded to Notting Hill and Portobello Road. We had our photos taken at the Notting Hill Bookstore, where Julia Roberts and Hugh Grant met, and his apartment's famous blue door. We even had *halo-halo* (a Filipino ice desert) at *Lakwatsa*, a Filipino pub.

But the very first friend I had met was a fellow sponsor at the University of the Philippines ROTC Corps of Sponsors some 47 years before. A member of London's Royal Academy of the Arts, she took me to the famed Ai Weiwei art exhibit that was going on at the time. After the tour, we had a brief stop at the British Museum, her apartment close by, and Covent Garden for tea. We met another time to view the newest attraction of London, the fabulous Sky Garden on the thirty-fifth to thirty-seventh floors. That is where you can get an unobstructed view of the Shard Building, the tallest building in London, the London Bridge, the Tower Bridge, and the Tower of London. We completed our visit with a walk to St. Paul's Cathedral, where Prince Charles and Princess Diana were married, a walk over the Millennium Bridge, a view of Shakespeare's Globe Theater on the left, a visit to the Tate Modern on the right, and scones, clotted cream, and tea at the Café inside.

And then Bill had some good news. We had about 5,000 points left in our time-share that we had to use before the end of the year. When I looked online, there was a one-bedroom unit available at Cromer Country Club in the Norfolk Coast Area. On Kyrie's one-month birthday, we drove the three-and-a-half-hour trip for a one-week vacation by the sea. Unfortunately, we were met by very English wet, cold and windy days. It was good there was a clubhouse with a fitness center, indoor heated pool, and sauna and steam baths.

On the fifth day the sun was shining, and we happily brought mother and son to town to see the beautiful stone cathedral and the famous Cromer Pier, the gem of the Norfolk coast and winner of the Pier of the Year 2015 award. It was certainly the prettiest beach town and pier I have seen in our travels around the UK.

On the sixth day, the sun was again shining. So we took the little boy around Cromer Country Club and discovered a hill beyond it. Atop the hill were a helipad, the lighthouse and lighthouse keepers' cottage, and the best view of the whole town. With the peeking autumnal (somebody pointed out to me that it isn't called fall in England, but autumn) colors, everything was picture perfect, including our villa, the garden, and the Virginia creepers.

What a great month I had as a Nanny in London. You may have noticed, I did not forget the traveler in me. But I would surely miss my youngest baby boy. It's a good thing I would soon be traipsing around seven countries in Europe with my BFF and then do a two-week Mexican vacation with Bill. Perhaps that will be enough until I reemerge as a Nanny in Melbourne. April's wish to become a UK immigrant was dashed by a technicality. That made her the US and UK's big loss. And now she is Australia's huge gain.

Just Keeping Him Company

After the divorce from my second husband and babysitting my first grandson in Calgary, I moved back to Seattle to take care of my second grandson Kenji, born six months later than Enzo. There I began to settle into another chapter of my life. At first I was just a nanny, but other interests crept in. By the time Bill rescued me from this other driven period of my life, I had been taking care of my grandson for two years in addition to all my other responsibilities. My life had again become sixty-hour workweeks.

Since then I have welcomed every chance to visit Seattle. I got a wonderful opportunity when Trisha, my eldest, needed a mother's help. My son-in-law Deejay had taken a new post with the City Engineer's Office in Livermore, California. She was supposed to follow, but she had to complete her IT scholarship at a community college, facilitating her move from the banking to the IT industry. In the meantime, before the new school year began, my grandson (just nine at the time) could not be left alone at home—ten year-olds can—while his mom worked and studied. His two older sisters were already away: the eldest, my first *Apo* (first grandchild) was already working as a hairstylist at a popular salon in Santa Monica, California; the second was completing her BS in Biology at the University of Washington.

But he was no longer a boy. Thus it was not really babysitting, but keeping him company. All I had to do for my daughter was to make sure he ate well, got his exercise outdoors, and was not too glued to his iPad. In fact, because he was old enough, I was able to bring him with me when I got the chance to visit with friends I had made in the city when I had lived there. While doing that, I got to see parts of Seattle that I had not seen before and to understand why Seattle has consistently ranked in the Top Fifty US Cities.

One of those visits was a trip to Bremerton on the Kitsap Peninsula, to the charming home of my Filipina friend from the St. John the Baptist Parish Church Filipino-American Association. Our husbands had helped found the group with several other Filipino couples and friends around Seattle.

The trip finally gave me the chance to ride the ferry; it was Kenji's first, too. Upon our arrival, they brought us to one of the most unusual museums we had ever visited. The Bug Museum completely surprised us. Giant spiders decorated the walls, and there were insects that you could not tell from their surroundings, dry leaves, twigs, or rocks. There was also a small reptile section where I shuddered at the sight of a huge Albino Burmese Python on display. It was a surprising rare time when the color yellow got me to cringe instead of smile.

At their lovely home we were served an all-American lunch that Kenji greatly enjoyed. But it was the view from their spacious deck that had me mesmerized. Even though there were scattered rain showers, grayish clouds were hovering around, and Mt. Rainier was in hiding, the deck looked out to the Puget Sound, an inlet of the Pacific Ocean. It is a system of interconnected marine waterways and basins, and the second largest estuary in the US behind the Everglades in Florida.

I found out later that my grandson had told his mom he was quite apprehensive about the ferry ride, of going too near the edge of the vessel and possibly falling overboard. That must have been the reason why, on the one-hour sailing to Bremerton, he had been completely focused on the mini-Lego blocks he had brought with him, finishing one complex design during the whole trip. On the way home he relaxed, walked out on the ship's deck, and we finally had a ball taking selfie photos with views of the Bremerton harbor, ferries that were sailing on Puget Sound, the different islands around it, and the Seattle skyline as we approached the city.

It was a day well spent with my grandson. I wished Bill had been with me. I'd seen Seattle from the water, but I realized it was not just being able to see a place from a different perspective. It wasn't just seeing old friends again. It was not even that I was able to take care of a grandchild, not as a baby, but as a growing person. The best part was that my daughter had given me another chance at helping her.

THROUGH HER MILLENNIAL EYES

Later Trisha and her family settled well into the San Francisco Bay area. I have been to the area many times but, since there are many Filipino friends and family in the different cities and towns, our visits have mostly been centered on social events. We had not really had a closer look at what makes the city such a top destination for tourists around the world.

In the summer of 2019 however, my twenty-three-year-old granddaughter Daniela—she had graduated from the University of Washington by then—was already working as a scientist in a pioneer biotech firm in the valley. In fact, she is now making test kits for coronavirus and considered an essential worker in their laboratory, not able to work from home.

She volunteered to take this elderly couple (Bill and me) around San Francisco. It meant the world to me that her big special millennial eyes, those that I had the pleasure of seeing as a baby, then as a young girl, as a teenager, and as a college student, saw fit to design the most beautiful two days we have ever had in the City by the Bay.

She introduced us to the mechanics of going around a city using Uber. Up to that time, I didn't even have the app installed on my phone, and it was a giant leap to be updated. First stop was Pier 39 with its many points of interest—the floral door, the Carousel Ride, the boardwalk, exotic shops, the artsy giant heart, and the great bay views. But when the barks, honks, grunts, growls, roars, moans or whatever else they call those sounds grew more loudly, we knew we were approaching the pier's highlight: the seals that for years have made it home. I had so much fun photographing the whole pod, including one playful one trying to be the star of the show.

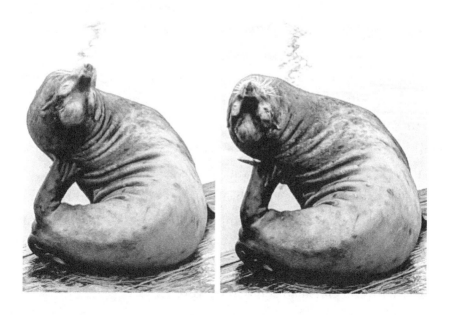

Pier 39 is one of the attractions of the famous neighborhood called Fisherman's Wharf. On the walk around this area, we spotted good street art, a great view of Alcatraz, and old WWII ships on display. But it is best known for the crabs, clam chowder on sourdough bread, and other seafood offered by the restaurants that have been serving visitors for generations. On the way to Ghirardelli Square and some chocolates and ice cream, we missed the view of the Golden Gate Bridge at the San Francisco Maritime Historical Park. It was hiding behind fog that day.

Another Uber ride took us to Chinatown. After the Dragon Gate, an area bustling with shoppers seeking all kinds of cultural products from the East—home décor, gadgets, souvenirs, produce, baked goods, dry goods, etc., at unbelievably low prices for San Francisco—unfolded before us. There were also plenty of cocktail and karaoke bars and food joints. Festive red balloons hung over the streets, making for great photos; so did the ornate buildings and temples. My granddaughter knew where to take us to buy the favorite Chinese food I had missed. One of them, Good Mang Kok, was the best bakery for cheap, awesome dim sums. No wonder this Chinatown is one of the oldest and best established in the US.

After lunch and another Uber ride, she took us to a place I never even knew existed. It's her favorite place for buying make-up for her Asian complexion. Japantown is a sprawling two-wing, two-level mall of everything Japanese—décor, gadgets, clothing, art, food, cosmetics, etc. I loved the giant pagoda at the entrance, the huge mural of colorful Japanese umbrellas, the red Japanese bridge connecting two floors, Japanese temple replicas, and other instagrammable spots. But the other reason she loved Japantown was matcha ice cream. She took us to a store that sold many different flavors. I stayed with the classic green tea, however.

The next day, our "fashionista' millennial urged us to discover what a major fashion center San Francisco truly is. We sought out Uniqlo—whose brand ambassadors include tennis icons Djokovic and Federer—to see what all the fuss is about this Japanese clothing brand. I found out that the secret is the brand's great designs and materials. We also visited JINS, the fashion eyeglass outlet frequented by millennials. I found some styles for me—at 71, I still felt 31. It is just too bad we do not have these stores in Phoenix. The variety of what is available is what I miss about Manila and other huge metropolitan centers.

During our shopping spree we walked through Union Square, and loved the Filipino flag hanging over one of the buildings fronting it. The flags of many other countries also hung on buildings, but they were a little farther away. We even found another artsy giant heart. Nearby was The Cable Car Turnaround, where the world-famous vintage trolleys turn around. The lines were too long, however, and we did not get the chance to hop on.

After lunch we visited the office of my youngest daughter April, herself also a millennial, who was in training at the Zendesk HQ. Actually, she was the reason we were all gathered in San Francisco at that time. The company is one of the most successful in innovative customer service apps and support. In fact, the giants Uber and AirBnb are two of its biggest clients. It was a delight to see how employee-centric the company is—probably why it is such a success.

With the optimal working environment the company provides, the creativity of every employee is unleashed. Modern food and bar areas are on every floor with pantries filled. There are nooks for every size and kind of discussion—in just twos, or in bigger groups, and even a huge dedicated creative studio. There are desks and chairs for every kind of working arrangement—including standing up or slouching with a laptop (my favorite position). San Francisco is one of the best workplaces in the world. Two other San Francisco-based companies, Google and Facebook, are leaders in this kind of workplace revolution. It was just coming into vogue when I was retiring from corporate life.

San Francisco is also a great place for dining. In fact, we enjoyed several big meals with April and Daniela. The highlight was our dinner at Crustacean, a sister restaurant of Thanh Long, the classic Vietnamese restaurant that has long served the famous roasted crab with garlic noodles sought out by many from all over the world. It was a friend from the Philippine computer industry who took me and my young girls there in the 1990s. They gushed then that it was the best meal they had ever had anywhere in the world and they had often dreamed of going back. We topped off the night with delectable Thai desserts at Kin Khao, right across from her hotel, Parc 55, where we also spent our second night, hearts happy and tummies filled.

We were able to give my youngest daughter company while she was visiting, and we definitely had a highly focused two days in San Francisco with the best tour guide I could ever dream of having. Daniela lives in Livermore, about forty-five minutes away, with her parents and brother, and she truly knew San Francisco well. It feels amazing that, after taking care of them off and on from birth, my grandchildren have begun to find ways of taking care of us.

In fact, my two millennial granddaughters had just vacationed with us in the mountain city resort of Big Bear Lake in California. Krishna and her fiancé had treated us to a visit at the Alpine Zoo and Daniela had hosted dinner at the only lakefront dining in town, Pines Lakefront. Life has indeed come full circle. It feels like a great privilege to reach this stage of life. As a matter of fact, Krishna is getting married in October 2021. It will not be long until I will again be promoted, this time to the highest position anyone can ever hope for in life: a pretty cool great grandmother.

6

FINDING A SECOND HOME

§

My infatuation with America began when I was very young. My father was a soldier who zealously fought alongside Americans on Philippine soil against the Japanese in WWII. My mother was a special education teacher who was sent to America on a year-long Philippine government scholarship to study and bring back to the country the latest in the education of the deaf. They both told me endless stories about the beautiful land across the Pacific and her lovely people. They infected me with their love for America.

The attraction was left largely unchecked. My getting a high school scholarship to the International School in the Manila only incensed it. After college, training by American multinationals—among them NCR, IBM, and SGV-Andersen Consulting—further deepened it. In fact, I briefly tested it when Philippine democracy and economy were in shambles after the fall of Marcos. But my children were still too small at the time so I had to go back. It was, therefore, no accident that I came to America to retire. And on Valentines' Day 2011, I became a US citizen.

BECOMING AN AMERICAN

Very early in our RV cruising days we started visiting spectacular national parks; and I was increasingly smitten by the beauty of America and frequently hummed America the Beautiful. When we started our drive up the east coast from Florida, however, the other reason for loving America became much clearer. The solemn landmarks in Washington DC and the places where the American flag and national anthem were born in Baltimore, Maryland told me about the making of this great nation. So I began to hum the Star-Spangled Banner, too.

In Philadelphia, I stood in awe in front of the Carpenters Hall where the first Continental Congress and the vote to wage war upon the British was held, the house where Thomas Jefferson crafted the Declaration of Independence, Independence Hall where the Constitution was signed, and the symbol of it all with its iconic crack, the Liberty Bell. In Boston and Concord, there were many historic sites where the American Revolution started to sizzle, fighting the initial skirmishes and firing the "shot heard round the world."

I was, in no uncertain terms, starting to feel like an American. I noticed feeling sad when I walked along the historic paths of strife and terror, happy when I reached the points of triumph and celebration, and inspired amid ancient ruins and great houses of Native Americans. How lucky could I be for having been accepted as a naturalized American citizen?

But I knew the conversion was complete when I began to feel pride. The technical difference between a US permanent resident and a naturalized citizen is that the latter can vote (or run for an elected office). I cast my vote for the very first time in the 2012 presidential elections via guaranteed express mail delivery. Then the country of more than 300 million accepted the results with polling centers in Hawaii and Alaska still open. It was amazing to watch how the Electoral College system helped determine the winners with such speed. And I know that speed is the best way to guarantee the safety of the will of the people. The year 2020, however, was kind of different largely as a result of the pandemic.

Aside from the electoral process, I just love the public library system. They say that there are more libraries than McDonalds' diners in America. Throughout our eight years of RVing, every county issued library cards to us even if we would only be in the area for a couple of weeks. We were also the most direct beneficiaries of the largest national highway system in the world, almost four million miles of overpasses and freeways that extend from coast to coast, seamlessly interconnecting with the city, county, and state roads.

Through Bill's $10 (now $80) Senior Golden Pass, we visited, for free, thirty-two of forty-nine National Parks, thirty-one of eighty-five National Monuments, and over a hundred other specially designated sites. I have also been to thirty of the forty-five American Presidents' homes, tombs, and/or presidential libraries; even to those of some of the great first ladies. We have come across memorials to other larger-than-life heroes, brave pioneers, cultural icons, and lay and church leaders. When we visited homes or museums of people who came to America and lived their own American dreams, I was greatly inspired. And visits to the homes and tombs of literary greats gave me the best nudge to begin and keep on writing.

We have been to the largest and the smallest of towns, the poorest of counties, and the wealthiest of states, and everything in between. Some of America's man-made structures and natural formations are among the tallest, biggest, longest, etc. in the world. There are features that you cannot find anywhere else. We visited factories of products made in America, and of noble institutions that serve the world. As a matter of fact, it was cool to read "A Quirky Tour of the US" in the *Readers' Digest* July 2014 issue. We had been to three of the six suggested places. Come to think of it, I have now slept in every single state.

My American education was a transfusion, not just an injection. I was forever changed. Travel made it all happen. RVing made it all so easy. I am no longer just a Filipino tourist, no longer a permanent resident. I am not even just a naturalized citizen. I am truly an American.

FINDING OUR PLACE IN THE SUN

In 2013, after considering Florida and Southern California and looking extensively in Arizona, we selected the latter as a place to stay put during winters. After looking at various campgrounds and resorts around the Phoenix area, we chose Viewpoint in Mesa, part of the Phoenix SMSA.

Doing this enabled us to establish our health support system in the state that is #5 in healthcare—and perhaps #1 in geriatric care— in the country. From this base, we went on American road trips and flew to other countries in Asia, Central America, Europe, and Africa. When we were out of the country, we kept the RV at a storage facility. It was incredible experiencing other cultures and traveling farther distances. Our travel lifestyle had changed. It had stepped up a notch.

We began to make many great friendships, more stable ones than those we found in RV campgrounds where we had to leave just as we had gotten close to some of the people. We warmed into the winter lifestyle, literally and figuratively. The season is when many like-minded people converge on Arizona—from the northern American states and Canada—looking for the sun. That is what snow-birding is all about and probably why the resort lifestyle was born. We bought into it big-time as the next step after cruising in an RV for five years.

LIVING THE RESORT LIFESTYLE

In 2017, after having wintered with our RV in Viewpoint for four years, I turned 69. Tired from being on the road for eight months, we took a meaningful pause. It became a turning point. We canceled our traditional Christmas gifts for each other, and instead we bought a cute three bedroom, brand new home in Viewpoint near its new Fitness and Leisure Center and golf courses. The transition into another phase of our travel life became complete.

We decided that our trips would consist firstly of visits to our children during the sizzling summer months. We also planned to use the sixteen timeshare weeks we own elsewhere around the world. Thus, this new travel lifestyle would divide our year into traveling and relaxation months. It was a ratio of almost 12:0 when we were RVing in 2009-2013. It dropped to 8:4 in 2013-2017 when we wintered in Viewpoint. Beginning in 2018, it has dropped further to 6:6 (this year it was just 4:8 because of the pandemic).

The months after we bought our "home base" were dizzying and exhilarating. It was truly our first home together. We briefly spent time at my condo in Seattle right after getting married, and he had rented out his condo-duplex. But we left for our epic RVing only six months later, also renting mine out. Buying and furnishing a home together was a brand new experience. It was fun, choosing furniture, appliances, accessories and décor. But sometimes there were conflicts as we tried to fit everything together into a look we BOTH liked. Believe it or not, he carried me over the threshold. What an experience to have at our age.

I must admit though that, as we packed our down-sized belongings and prepared the RV for sale, we felt a certain kind of sadness. It dawned on me that the RV period of my life was exceptionally rare, not just for an American, but more so for a Filipino in America. After all, the cozy home that was our RV was where—as I wrote in *Carolina: Cruising*—I "not only learned to be a wife without losing my identity but also to be an American without losing my roots."

It was a pleasant surprise that we sold the RV at noon of the same day we put out the ad on Craigslist. Perhaps our asking price was too low. But it quickly enabled us to turn to planning the different kind of travel we would have from then on. None of our children live near each other, and we both love too many other places in the world to stay put. But, first, I enjoyed a month and a half of living in a home not propped up on wheels. We had moved from 350 square feet of space to 1,200. My prayer was that that I would not get lost.

To best describe this resort lifestyle, allow me to completely list the facilities available at Viewpoint: two golf courses with a clubhouse that has a golf-pro shop, a restaurant/bar/grille, a ballroom and a smaller party room; a main clubhouse with two swimming pools, three hot tubs, a sauna, hobby and craft rooms, a billiards room, a computer room, a laundry room, a beauty salon, two ballrooms, and shuffleboard courts; a third clubhouse with a swimming pool and two hot tubs, a sauna, a fitness center, a dance studio, a laundry room, a card room, and four meeting rooms. The newest gathering area is the Fitness and Leisure Center— walking distance from our home, about eight houses away—that contains a gym, a huge pool and hot tub and two party areas. There is also a ball field, ten tennis courts, ten pickle ball courts, and a wood work- shop building on the grounds.

During the height of the season, about fifty clubs operate to serve various interests. While Bill plays golf or tennis or takes walks, I busy myself with the Technology Group, the Photography Club, and the Author's Forum. I also usually join Karaoke Night on Mondays, Poker Night on Tuesdays, Scrabble Afternoons on Thursdays, and Forever 39 Happy Hour on Fridays.

The Resort also hosts weekly dances, concerts, dinners, and other thematic activities during the snow birding season. During off-season, Viewpoint's full-time residents—now numbering about six hundred—has a committee of residents which hosts an activity on most days. In fact, during the pandemic, we hosted Zoom par- ties for our friends and neighbors. If you ever feel lonely or bored in Viewpoint, it would be your own fault. In fact, if you don't keep a detailed calendar, you will likely miss a few events.

This lifestyle fits very well into our travel plans. Whereas we traveled full-time before, now we carve out spring and fall when the desert weather is best to relax and renew relationships. Our travels during summer are designed to escape the desert heat. That is when we visit our children and grandchildren in colder areas—Calgary, San Francisco, Melbourne, Anchorage, Boise, and Denver. That is the time we also use our month of timeshare points in Europe or elsewhere around the world. Now that we have another three months of all-inclusive timeshare in Mexico, we spend our winters there at an El Cid Resort in Mazatlan, Cancun or Cozumel as "snowbirds from Phoenix." I know; it's a bit of an oxymoron.

Last year, we arrived back in Arizona from Mexico on April 3, staying at home for three months before our two road trips of two and six weeks each to six American states and two Canadian provinces. After the two trips and a quick flight to San Francisco for a four-day weekend, we stayed put for another three months. It was our first year of staying at home for all of seven months, three in spring, a few broken weeks in summer, and three in fall.

This year was even "worse." Because of the coronavirus pandemic, we had to return ten days early from Mexico, on March 23. We were on lockdown until May 23, canceled our April trips, and loved that we had a great home where we could self-isolate in comfort. Only the outdoor sports facilities were kept open, so we went to state, regional, and national parks for natural social distancing and discovered many small Arizona towns with character. We resumed our travels in July and August to mountain retreats in Utah, Colorado, and California. And we are planning to resume our schedules in January with winter in Mexico.

Did this active traveler in her seventies give in to boredom and accumulate pounds? The answer is a resounding "NO!" Viewpoint has everything you need for an active 55+ lifestyle. There are also the very engaging activities of cooking our favorite dishes, tending to my plants, and shopping for the home. And when it becomes possible, we hope to return to the practice of hosting valued friends at our home, serving Filipino cuisine, and deepening bonds.

One of the biggest benefits of having a home is that you get visits from family and friends. In 2018, we had two, both from Bill's side of the family. My eldest daughter and her family visited last year. So did my sisters and two friends. Each time, we got the chance to show our guests why we chose to settle in this area. Especially for Bill's eldest daughter and her daughter, whose life goal (one of them) is to visit as many national parks and monuments as possible, we showed them as many as we could in two days.

We are waiting for her return because we have expanded our original list to include Antelope Canyon, Horseshoe Bend, and the Glen Canyon National Recreation Area. There are also the large Indian reservations to the east, with the Petrified National Forest and Meteor Crater Natural Landmark, Lake Havasu and the London Bridge to the west, and to the southwest, Yuma and more national monuments.

Besides all these sights, there are many places to explore in the surrounding cities of Phoenix, Scottsdale, Tempe, Chandler, Gilbert, and Apache Junction all have markets, festivals, theater, opera, movies, and other activities galore all year-round. We don't rush to go to everything they all have to offer because we know we have ample time to see them when the time comes that we no longer are able to travel to more distant places.

But the biggest benefit of having a home is that I am able to be relatively still for some time. I get enough time for blogging and social media with lots of rest in between. It is also the time we have our biennial medical check-ups and get reassured we are okay. This time between travels has no ups and downs. There is a lot of stability in my environment and I get to follow an established routine. It's comfortable because it's home. There's something restorative in sleeping in my own bed, watching my own TV, and eating food that I have cooked myself.

This time allows me to be renewed for the hectic and exciting travel days ahead. I don't think I would be able to bounce around for six weeks straight on a great North American road trip, or for five weeks straight of exciting rail travel in Europe, if we didn't have the downtime. It's time to be refreshed. My travel juices are focused on planning future trips, researching remaining bucket list items, and choosing among competing alternatives and finding the best deals.

The same downtime gives me the necessary space to wonder about our wanderings. I find that it gives me moments when I get not only the time, but the inspiration to write articles with deeper perspectives. That's how this book was born.

I also feel healthier during this downtime. Fitbits have become our constant companions. A Charge 3 rests nicely on my left wrist; it constantly tells me how well I slept and how much I moved every day. During our last three months in Mexico, I slept an average of six hours and walked 7-9,000 steps a day, was at the Fitness and Spa Center daily, and ate hearty meals at three of the nine all-inclusive restaurants every day. Okay, I gained three pounds.

At our Viewpoint home, I sleep the same number of hours and visit the fitness center each day (or a video exercise routine during the time of Covid). However, since I do not have to walk from building to building to get to restaurants and activities, my daily steps are just 4-5,000. But then I also do not eat a lot. First of all, the meals I cook are not as fabulous. Neither do I want to cook more. So, I have lost the pounds I gained in Mexico.

A well-thought-out, well-spent downtime between trips and adventures is heaven-sent. Being home gets me renewed. I am glad we have it at least half of the year. Even the three months in Mexico is almost like it (and will be more and more like it). Viewpoint is indeed a great base for travels; our place under the Arizona sun is ideal for travelers at this age. Perhaps, since we have a home base, loved ones can visit us more than we visit them. It all comes together as cruising past seventy.

7

REKINDLING THE FILIPINO

It was a happy day when I took my oath as an American citizen in Seattle. But I must admit there was ambivalence. That is because I had to renounce my Filipino citizenship at the same time. It was one of those difficult decisions one has to make in life. At the time, I had been in the US for seven years. And in the last three of those years after I married Bill, especially while RVing, I had begun to sorely miss the many things I enjoyed back home. As a matter of fact, the newly launched Philippine tourism slogan at the time, "It is more fun in the Philippines," magnified the feeling even more.

I was fifty-four when I retired and left to migrate to America. The Philippines is where I had spent most of my life, where I grew up, where I received all of my education, where I enjoyed a great career, and where I gave birth to all of my children. Memories of my life there will never leave my heart. I have two sisters, and many long-time friends who still live there. So I visit whenever I can. I have proudly showed Bill the land from where I came in three of my four visits in the last twelve years. One of them is included as a vignette here.

At first I did not notice the changes going on inside me as my husband took me RVing across America. When my dancing changed from disco and ballroom to country and rock, I took a little pause but went on. When my cuisine changed from cooking *adobo* (pork stewed in garlic, vinegar and soy sauce), *pancit* (stir-fry noodles with vegetables) and *lumpia* (vegetable egg rolls) to grilling burgers and hot dogs and baking pies, I actually began to be somewhat alarmed. As I started to feel proud of America's beauty, history, and accomplishments, guilt entered my psyche.

Although Bill says I hardly have an accent, I readily shifted to Tagalog whenever I was with fellow Filipinos. In fact, I still think in Tagalog and feel more at ease speaking in my native tongue. I still think a sandwich is not a meal because it doesn't involve rice. Naturally, I also think that *pan de sal* (bread) is only for snacks or breakfast. No cosmetic will ever erase the fact that my skin is brown and my nose is small. But neither do I want to change any of those things.

When Megan Young was crowned Miss World, I beamed with pride because the Philippines emerged as the only country that has won all five of the most coveted global beauty titles—Miss Universe, Miss International, Miss Earth, Miss World, and Miss Globe International. Some titles even had several Filipinas on their roster. For me, it means that the universal standard of feminine beauty is no longer defined by the color of a woman's skin or the fineness of her features. By the same token, I readily commiserated with the many Filipinos I met around the world who have been working hard, making the great sacrifice of not being with their families, eking out dollars to send them. Pride in Filipino triumph and compassion for Filipino sacrifices will always be automatic impulses for me.

The cultural tension would ease when I remembered the deep kinship between the Philippines and America. We share the Pacific Ocean and with it, the treacherous Pacific Ring of Fire. Spain colonized the American Southwest and the Philippines during the same period of about three hundred years. In fact, both territories, not coincidentally, were ceded to America when she won the Spanish-American and the Mexican-American Wars. Today, countless Filipino nurses, teachers, and seamen are an integral part of US hospitals, schools, and ships. July 4 is now doubly meaningful to me. In 1946, the US gave us our own independence on that day, 170 years after she got hers.

But I remain keenly aware of the differences. The Philippines is a tropical archipelago of 7,641 islands while the US is more of a

201

vast contiguous temperate land— except for Hawaii and a few other islands near its western and eastern coastlines. Flora and fauna are different. When I step into the wide vistas of the Great Plains, the desert landscape of the southwest, and the glaciers of Alaska, it is a world far from what I knew as a child. The Filipino can easily be pictured while the American has become so diverse. Filipinos are clannish, Americans generally more private. And infrastructure and social systems in America are so much more developed. But the Philippines is only seventy-four years old; the US, already 244. There is time and room for my homeland to grow.

From the time I received my American citizenship, my heart had been heavy with understandable guilt. But I knew I would wake up sooner or later. Las Vegas, Nevada proved to be the turning point. That's where the Filipino in me was rekindled. That's where I was able to taste near-forgotten favorite Filipino food cooked for me by a cousin, to enjoy talking in Tagalog with former Filipino colleagues, and to review much-missed Filipino traditions like the Santacruzan that is celebrated there annually by its strong Filipino community.

It was also in Las Vegas that I found out that the Philippines is one of the forty-two countries for which the US allows dual citizenship. I jumped with joy, for a moment, until I found out that there was no Philippine Consulate where I could apply for it in Phoenix, Arizona. The nearest one was six hours away in Los Angeles, California. It meant I had to wait a little while longer.

On October 3, 2013, I made that special trip to LA, two years after I obtained my US citizenship. There I re-pledged my loyalty to my native land and became a Filipino-American. I did not, so to speak, get melted in the pot. Instead, I got included in a colorful chunky stew, contributing to the taste but retaining my own shape, color, and flavor. From this privileged perch, I see my developing homeland from the perspective of my developed country. My mission is clear, therefore: it is for me to help the Philippines as an American while I contribute to America as a Filipino.

MANONG AND HIS JEEPNEY

Aside from describing what makes it "more fun in the Philippines" as a great destination, this story tries to describe what the secret is behind the claim. Many will agree with me that the basics of a great trip are spectacular scenes, extraordinary adventures, and an intimate peek at an unfamiliar way of life. There is one other factor, however, that makes a trip stand out. I discovered it when I took Bill on his first visit to my home country.

Despite the thirty-year age difference, our connection with Jure and Katarina from Slovenia was immediate. Bill and I met them on a tour of the Puerto Princesa Subterranean River, the world's longest navigable underground river on the island of Palawan, Philippines. This island had consistently been named "the best island in the world" several years in a row. It is in the Visayas, the island group in the middle of the country.

While sampling crocodile *sisig* at the popular Kinabuch Grill, we told the Slovenians to avoid going south to Mindanao, the second largest island in the country. Parts of it are alleged to be training grounds of Islamic extremists. But we agreed to accompany them on a trip to the amazing rice terraces of northern Luzon, the largest island to the north, and breathe clean Philippine mountain air.

We slept most of the seven-hour night bus ride from Manila to Banaue, where the famous rice terraces are carved into the Cordilleras, the region's mountain range. When we felt the whiff of cold air on our faces and smelled the fresh scent of pines, we knew we had arrived in the municipality of Banaue in the province of Ifugao (population, 22,000).

Bill and Jure carried our bags up the uneven wooden stairs to our rooms on the third floor of the modest mountain chalet while Katarina and I remained to negotiate with a short, dark, wrinkled mountain man. He was an Igorot—what Ifugao people are called—and was intensely chewing betel nuts wrapped in leaves, sitting in the token dining area behind the reception desk.

"Jeepney, Ma'am?" he asked. He was referring to a vestige of America's WWII presence. The jeeps have been extended and colorfully decorated by locals, and have become the norm for getting around all over the country. I said, *"Manong, hindi kami mayaman."* I used the local term for an elderly man and explained we didn't have lots of money. Hearing the ongoing negotiations, a Spanish couple, three male foreign students, and a Dutch couple soon came in. Satisfied with the rate I had negotiated, they all joined us on the two-day tour.

Manong took us first to the nearby Banaue Rice Terraces. It was a spectacular sight, soaring over 5,000 feet into the sky. These "stairways to heaven" were carved by the Igorots with their own bare hands, probably 2,000 years ago. They were built to create better fields for planting rice, their staple food. Banaue, together with the other less accessible rice terraces called Batad, Mayoyao, Hapao, and Kiangan, are collectively classified as UNESCO's first cultural World Heritage Site.

On the way to Batad, we encountered a jeepney so packed that people were clinging to its side rails and sitting atop its roof. There must have been twenty people where only ten should have been. Intrigued, Jure climbed to the top of our vehicle and called down, "The view is better from up here!" As expected, Manong deftly negotiated the one-lane mud road marked with deep ruts. The ride became an adventure in itself. A few of us thought we would never make it. But we did.

At the end of the road, Manong parked his jeepney and led us to the forty-five-minute descent on foot to Batad. There were wooden slats at first, but later they disappeared. Parts of the path were almost vertical. Bill and I, older than the others, fell more and more behind. Finally, we caught up, breathed pure, clean mountain air, and beheld the jewel that was Batad. The village was a cluster of huts at the middle and bottom of the glistening terraces that radiate upwards around them. Only a few get to Batad; those who do are hugely rewarded.

The next day Manong was early for our trip to Sagada, the other pride of the Cordilleras. At the cusp of a U-shaped portion of the narrow mountain pass, however, we had to stop. A landslide that had occurred earlier prevented the jeepney from going forward. Manong immediately shouted to another driver on the other side to take care of us. He and his jeepney stayed behind. Luckily, there were city engineers on site. They helped us cross the fallen boulders, looking down a steep drop-off. That was the scariest walk of our lifetime.

Another Manong and a new jeepney took us straight to the hanging coffins, a traditional way of burying Igorots who are held in high respect, been married, fathered children, and had grandchildren. There were several sites at Echo Valley where we saw them from afar. But at Sumaguing "Burial" Cave, we saw them up close. The coffins were hung all over the sides of the cave. That was a unique experience for all of us.

There were many Igorots who had been following us as we roamed the center of Sagada, a municipality of 12,000 people in the Mountain Province. In their broken English, they told us about a not-to-miss adventure: a cave connection trip where the brave can enter Sumaguing and come out of Lumiang Cave, another burial site, on the other side. The men were intrigued. After I helped negotiate the fees for two guides, Bill and the other five men disappeared into the cave. The two other women and I decided to wait at the nipa hut by Sumaguing's mouth, sampling native rice cakes filled with caramelized coconut shreds we bought from a nearby makeshift store.

After more than a couple of hours, the men emerged, walking on the trail, dirty and tired, having come from Lumiang Cave on the other side of the mountain. "What an adventure!" they all shouted, telling us of the steep drops, small crevices, stark darkness, the bats and their droppings. But the clear highlight was the thirty-foot long water hole they had to swim across at the bottom of Sumaguing Cave to cross to Lumiang.

As luck would have it, on the way home we encountered another problem. A bulldozer working on the road across the small valley had broken down, stopping everyone on the way in and out of Sagada. As far as the eye could see, vehicles were lined up on both sides. "We have a flight back to Spain tomorrow," the Barcelona couple anxiously said.

We hurriedly paid our second Manong then walked to the line on the other side. There we found our third Manong, whose passengers were willing to exchange places with us. He turned around and took us back to the site of the morning landslide. When we got there, a pedestrian path had been cleared. On the other side, our original Manong and his jeepney were patiently waiting for us.

This adventure had all the basics that make a great trip. But what made it stand out was the people with whom we shared all the excitement. The foreigners we met have become lifelong friends. In fact, we have been to visit some of them in their homes, as they have ours. But it was the three Igorot Manongs who stole the show. They made us feel so well taken care of and gave us such great jeepney adventures. For me, however, there was an extra touch. It stands out especially because Bill got to know my country and said, "The Philippines is beautiful, the Filipino is even more beautiful, but my Filipina wife is the most beautiful."

8

FINDING A THIRD HOME

At the time of this writing, I had visited forty-eight countries, twenty-nine of them with Bill, thirteen with girlfriends, and six alone for business in my distant past. In all of these trips, I wasn't looking for a new home. I was looking for excitement, education, and enlightenment. It surprised me, therefore, that I would add another country to the two places I already consider home. Yes, Mexico has risen to almost the same status as the Philippines and the US.

We spent the Christmas season of 2018-19 in Cozumel, that charming Mexican island on the Caribbean. It was there where we were persuaded to upgrade our timeshare in Mexico to an all-inclusive stay at any of seven resorts in Cozumel, Cancun, or Mazatlan. So, from January to March of 2019, and then again in 2020, we spent our winters in Mexico. These are the months when it is just got too cold for me in Phoenix.

Mexico, in particular Mazatlan, is Bill's dream retirement home and, at first, I acceded to this arrangement as a compromise. But now there are many reasons why it feels like home to me, too. As a matter of fact, we can't wait to go back this January, if and when it will be considered safe and the ban on non-essential travel between the US and Mexico is lifted.

MY FIRST IMPRESSIONS OF MEXICO

Twelve years ago we made our first trip to Mexico in our 24-foot Class B motorhome. Many had warned us of the woes and the hardships of doing this, but as newbies in traveling, nothing was going to stop us. So we bravely left the comforts of St. David Resort in Arizona and the warmth of new-found friends to spend the first month of our winter in Mexico.

When we were nearing the border, however, following some of the advice, I hurriedly removed mine and Bill's jewelry, save for our wedding bands. Bill thought I was being foolish to be affected by the horror stories. He says he had never had a problem in Mexico and felt safer there than even in some parts, neighborhoods, and cities of the US.

Surprisingly, the entry process only took two hours at Km 21, the visa center. With Bill's American passport and my green card— I would get my American citizenship two years later— the tourist permits took no time at all. The vehicle permits, however, took longer because of the complication brought about by Vino. We had planned not to use the scooter around Mexico, but we found out that we still needed a vehicle permit to bring it back into the USA.

Once we were back in the saddle, I sat back in great anticipation. We were to meet my children and grandchildren in Mazatlan, Mexico for my birthday, Thanksgiving, and a family reunion. We had not had a complete gathering for seven years, ever since we started to leave our Manila nest. But soon, the beautiful and vast Mexican countryside caught my attention.

First, agriculture in Mexico was so vibrant. The soil was very colorfully red, the weeds bright and golden, and the plants verdant green. And, although technologically not as advanced as American fields, they used many creative practices such as greenhouses, tarp coverings, irrigation canals, and crop dusters to protect the young and encourage the old plants, things I had not seen extensively used in Philippine fields. Growing beside the big US market must be a huge incentive for the farmers.

Second, Mexican religiosity was evident everywhere. "Chapelitas" or little chapels—built to remember those who died on those spots— dot the fields along the highways. They are small concrete structures; some can even hold two or three people, with an altar and a cross (es) either inside or out. The hillsides were painted with religious sayings and images; grottos and crosses were often erected on them. They were much more prevalent than what I had seen in the Philippines, which is also predominantly Catholic.

Third, RVing seemed practically dead in Mexico except for the occasional passing caravan. We used three parks: Sonora RV Park in Hermosillo, Los Mochis RV Park in Los Mochis, and Hotel Tres Rios Trailer Park in Culiacan. They all had spaces for about thirty or more RVs, had water, electric, and sewer hook-ups, WIFI connections, and flush toilets. Los Mochis even had hot showers. But they were eerily empty; we were the only game in town. It was sad to see.

One of the reasons could have been the onerous toll fees exacted regularly, frequently, and without fail. Up to Culiacan we had spent about $40 in fees at about six toll booths in about 600 miles. It practically doubled our daily camping fee of $20 a night. So we took the Mazatlan Libre (free) route instead of the Mazatlan Cuota (toll) route the next day. We found it slower, with only two lanes, and more pot-holes—yes, the toll roads had them, too—but more scenic.

211

But there are many other possible reasons why there was a lack of RVers venturing into Mexico. Maybe it was the flagging economy; or the continuing swine flu scare. There may even be the persistent perception of lack of safety due to drug crimes and other security issues. Whatever the reasons were, it was sad that the beauty of Mexico as a country and the warmth of its people were largely undiscovered, relatively underexplored, and quite underappreciated.

Despite all these negatives, there are many reasons why we loved our first winter in Mexico.

First, the people were wonderful. We were filling up at a Pemex gas station—all owned by the government, charging one price—in Culiacan when two brothers in a car went out of their way to lead us to our campground. Earlier, while we were trying to park at Ley, a grocery chain, a driver got out of his car to remove the carts that were in our way. All along the highways I felt like a celebrity because people constantly waved at us.

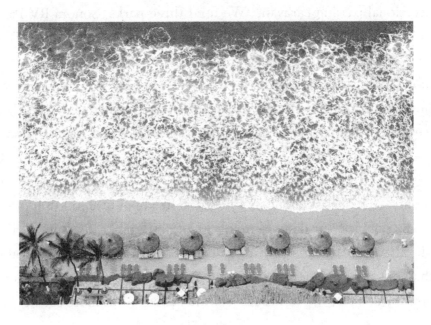

Then there is the weather. When we left St. David, it was 75 degrees in the day and 35 degrees at night. By 12 noon I would be walking in my bathing suit to the pool. By nightfall I would be looking for my sweater. In Mexico, days were in the eighties and nights, in the seventies. I went to the palapa near the beach for karaoke night, and ended up dancing the night away in the same strappy tank top and short shorts I wore in the afternoon.

And then there is the variety of things to do: shopping, eating out, and swimming. Zona Dorada, the golden zone, is like Santana Row in San Jose, State Road in Santa Barbara, or Palm Canyon Drive in Palm Springs, only very much more affordable. If you want to get vibrantly colorful Mexican craft and exquisite, intricate or bold, one-of-a-kind jewelry, this was the place to go. The whole family feasted at the good ole Shrimp Factory where *camarrones* (shrimp) were served in countless delicious ways. After all, Mazatlan is the "Shrimp Capital of the World." If you want cheaper food, there are many street food outlets. If you want fine dining, there are so many great restaurants, too. And there are beaches everywhere. In fact, the Mazatlan Malecon is the longest in Latin America.

Finally, there are the many Mexican landmarks of its unique history and culture, starting in Old Mazatlan with its Catedral, Mercado, Teatro, and Plazas. When we left Mazatlan, we did not go back to the US by the same route we came in. We wanted to go to Texas and Florida. So we went south through Guadalajara and proceeded to Teotihuacan, several kilometers north of Mexico City. The town hosts the community of ruins—the Pyramid of the Moon, the Jaguar Palace, the Avenue of the Dead, and the Pyramid of the Sun, the third largest pyramid of the world—which have all been meticulously restored, allowing us to better imagine the ancient Mayan civilization, and making us appreciate the grandeur of the oldest, most advanced culture in North America.

Then there was Ciudad de Mexico itself, probably the most populated (18 M) and, therefore, the most polluted city in the world. The Catedral Metropolitana is the oldest (1573) and largest cathedral in the Americas. It has four facades, twenty-five bells in its two towers, twelve chapels, etc. It is built on top of the Templo Mayor, the Aztec Ruins that lie below Mexico City. The Plaza de la Constitucion was across it and the Palacio Nacional was to its left. All around this historical wonder are shops and eateries for everyone's delight.

Historical sight-seeing in the city culminated with the visit to the famous park on Chapultepec (grasshopper) Hill where the Chapultepec Castle stands as one of only two royal palaces in North America. It is where the reigning Emperor, Maximillian I and his consort Empress Carlota lived during the Second Mexican Empire. It has now become the Museum of History of Mexico (Spanish and post-Spanish periods). The park also houses the Museo Antropologica which features the pre-Spanish period.

Despite these wonderful experiences, there were three that unsettled us. One, the Metro in Mexico City was so packed during rush hours, having to segregate men and women into different carriages, that I decided to take a fast and furious taxi ride through the congested city to our bus station. Two, Bill lost his cell phone in one of the many seas of humanity we encountered. Three, Bill caught pneumonia and was rendered quite ill for about ten days as soon as we reached Texas. As they warned, if you have a respiratory problem, do not go to Mexico City.

But the lingering thoughts of Mexico are these: sunny beaches, vibrant colors— on everything from churches to houses, tombs, dolls, jewelry, etc.; a polluted city, ancient ruins, endless fields; agave, cactus, and Joshua trees; friendly people, spicy food, *chapelitas, cuotas,* the Tropic of Cancer—like the Tropic of Capricorn in the south, it is he imaginary line where the sun is directly overhead at noon during the two solstices—and the *Ruta* 2010, the 2010 bicentennial celebration of independence from Spain and the Mexican Revolution in 1910. May you become as fascinated as I did during my first trip to Mexico.

FILIPINO-MEXICAN PARALLELS

Mexico and the Philippines share major parallels in history. Although we started with very different indigenous cultures, we were each ruled by Spain for centuries, Mexico for 300 and the Philippines for 377, both starting in 1521 at the height of the global Spanish empire. Thus, Spanish influence is heavy in both cultures. It is why we have many striking similarities.

First, ninety percent of both countries is Roman Catholic, although Mexico is bigger in population by 20 million, at 130 million. Therefore, one of the obvious comforts for us (Bill is also Catholic) is that we did not have a hard time finding churches around for Sunday mass. From our base in Mazatlan, there is one only half a mile (ten-minute walk) to the left and another, the same distance to the right. The only problem was the English masses are both at 8 am and I can't wake up early. The solution is to learn how to speak Spanish, which brings us to the next subject.

Second, Mexico is the largest Spanish-speaking country in the world. And lucky for me, many Tagalog words have their origin in Spanish, too: *silya* for *silla* (chair), *sapatos* for *zapatos* (shoes), *kamiseta* for *camiseta* (shirt), *banyo* for *baño* (bathroom), for example. I had relative ease carrying on a smattering of conversations even without learning the language formally. And I now have free formal classes every winter.

Third—and what I am thrilled about most—is that we share so many dishes. Mexican food is one of Bill's favorite foods, and he didn't have to find familiar foods to be happy. I initially thought Mexican cuisine was just tacos, fajitas, burritos, and enchiladas. Those are the "Gringoized" dishes, I discovered. I delighted in finding a lot of familiar favorites.

One of those is *chicharrones* (crispy pork rind), especially since they are almost always discarded after the pork meat is shredded for the *tacos de puerco*. I usually have most of the *chicharrones* to myself, as a matter of fact. Don Ignacio chicken could easily be mistaken for our chicken *inasal*. *Sopa de mariscos* is actually *sinigang* with shrimps or fish. I love to eat my *pescado frito* or *pritong isda* with a plate of fried garlic rice and sliced tomatoes. Even their grilled mahi-mahi, *pescado zarandeando* is similar to our *inihaw na bangus*. Finally for dessert, I always have the option of flan (just like our *leche flan*), candied *camote* or plantain banana, or the tropical fruits I have so missed. *Jicamas* (*singkamas* in Manila) have been mainstays in my salads, too. The only part of Filipino cuisine we do not share with Mexico is that which comes from our Chinese heritage. So I miss *pancit* and the various forms of *lumpia* when I am there.

Fourth, even music is shared due to our common Spanish heritage. I loved singing *Cucurucucu Paloma* when I found Lola Beltran's *Museo* in El Rosario, an hour south of Mazatlan. And I always sing or hum to *La Bamba, Besame Mucho, Sabor a Mi, or Cuando Caliente El Sol* whenever they are aired as piped-in music at any of the nine El Cid restaurants. But I have yet to participate in the Karaoke sessions. They start too late at 9 pm every night.

Fifth, festivals and traditions are very much alike: *Navidad (Pasko)*, *Dia de Los Muertos* (All Souls Day), and *Dia de Los Santos* (All Saints Day), for example. This year we had a *Feliz Ano Nuevo* (New Year's Eve) party at La Concha just two days after our arrival, complete with the same traditions of a fireworks display and eating of round fruits at midnight. Then on February 14, we had a party called *Dia del Amor y la Amistad* (Day of Love and Friendship). Filipinos celebrate these festivals with the same pomp, traditions, costumes, and props.

Sixth, both Mexicans and Filipinos are warm and expressive. Whenever Mexican manners are complimented, I tell people they should also go to the Philippines, and they will experience the same level of helpfulness and hospitality. We have many new friends, not just from the guests from Canada and America like us, but from the local staff of our resort. We have even been invited to their family parties and homes, just like Filipinos would when they meet visitors.

Seventh, our climates are so alike: sunny, warm, and humid. And our sunsets (and sunrises) are gloriously the same. Frolicking at the beaches is an everyday to-do in both countries. Because of this, we have many of the same great flora and fauna. I love the same blazing colors of the hibiscus and bougainvilla, and the towering palm and coconut trees. The seafood for both is fantastic although the shrimps of Mazatlan are legendary and humongous. But I still prefer the crabs in the Philippines, especially the *alimango* version.

Eighth, after the periods of Spanish rule, both of our histories became intertwined with the US. The Mexicans were defeated by the Americans in the Mexican-American War and Mexico ceded half of its territory to become the southwestern part of the US. The

Americans also defeated the Spanish in the Spanish-American War and Spain ceded the Philippines to the US in 1898. This began the 50-year rule of America over my native land until our independence was granted in 1946. We could say that, during this period, the Philippines developed contemporaneously, just like Mexico, with the southwestern US. Thus, it is not by chance that we have chosen to live in Arizona as our primary home and to make Mexico our second.

Filipinos, Mexicans, and Arizonans are truly brothers in history and culture. It's so good that I do not have to make the twenty-four-hour flight to Manila to be "home." Now in my seventies, it has become more difficult to do this. I will still visit the Philippines once every five years, perhaps. But today, I can just take the two-hour flight to somewhere in Mexico—in fact, we drive by car for just fifteen hours to reach Mazatlan— and I am also "home!"

9

TURNING GLOBAL

Having three homes requires me to travel to a lot of places regularly; not that I am complaining. But it is really my children who lead me everywhere. I love to visit my three daughters at least once a year and no two of them are in the same country at the same time. They don't always stay put in the same place, either.

My eldest Trisha lived in Seattle for many years, but now she lives in the Bay Area in Livermore, California. My second daughter Claudine has lived with her family in Calgary, Alberta since she left the Philippines. But my youngest April, who was left behind in our Manila home after I migrated to America, has cast her net wide. Her work assignments have taken her to the US, Spain, and the UK. And now she has chosen to make Australia home.

Visits to them have allowed us to explore the areas where they live. More importantly, however, they are opportunities for deepening our understanding and appreciation of life in different places because we usually stay longer in their homes. In a sense, they are homes to us, too. I have included in this chapter two vignettes on how

I have come to love two other countries, the UK and Australia—Canada has been covered extensively elsewhere in this book— that I have come to love because of those visits. They show how enjoyable and educational visits to loved ones always end up being, and how they are leading me to become a "global citizen."

WHY I WILL GO BACK TO THE UK IN A JIFFY

In 2013 the multinational company in the Philippines my youngest daughter April worked for assigned her to a huge IT project in the UK. Her four years there allowed me to visit all the countries that comprised the kingdom: Wales was incorporated in 1536, Scotland in 1707 and Ireland in 1801. In 1922, however, five-sixths of Ireland seceded to form the Republic of Ireland, leaving behind what is now known as Northern Ireland.

I was able to spend a total of four months in the UK. I got a pretty good idea why the couple loved the UK. In fact, I would go back there in a jiffy, and here are the ten reasons why:

1. One hallmark is the simple, good life. Examples are lines of small colorful cottages for changing along beaches, sturdy stone bridges over clear rivers, rolling farm meadows everywhere, herds of sheep grazing in grasslands, and pretty little English gardens.

2. There is a lot of precious history that is preserved in prehistoric, Roman, and religious ruins, venerable clock towers, imposing monuments, living cathedrals, and all kinds of castles that are in ruins or still in use.

3. The UK constantly reminds me of my favorite color combination, red and black. I miss those especially ubiquitous red phone booths, the big red hop-on-hop-off buses, and the classic, sleek, and spacious black cabs.

4. The great theater tradition established by the likes of Shakespeare *et al* continues to live on. I saw more plays, most of them outdoors, in my two months there than my previous five years in the US.

5. The UK ranks high on human development indicators, almost as high as the US, although not as good as the Scandinavian countries. People are generally happy and enjoy quality of life. The country is eighty-seven percent Caucasian, but that is fast changing.

6. The economy is very stable: it is the sixth-largest economy in the world and the third-largest in Europe, even as it exits the European Union. The tourism industry is a major part of the economy, along with oil and gas. The UK

ranks as the sixth major tourist destination in the world, and London is the city with the most international visitors. There are a lot of reasons why. Even in my favorite spectator sport of tennis, Wimbledon (in the outskirts of London) is the premier major tournament. I made it a point to go to the event.

7. Food supply is excellent. Every single fruit or vegetable I bought was deliciously sweet and fresh. Seafood is always great and available. I loved the pies, especially the pasties that were bigger versions of the Filipino empanada. But I simply went gaga over fruit scones and clotted cream. We had it every single day, and have searched far and wide to find some in the US. And I would not mind having High Tea every day; just not always at the Ritz.

8. The UK as energy-producer is ranked #43 in per capita carbon footprint vs. #12 USA, #32 Finland, and #33 Norway. She is definitely energy-efficient. Roads are very narrow, cars are very small, and people depend on public transport systems like the highly developed rail network. Homes are usually modest: thatched cottages and small stone homes in rural areas and walk-ups in the cities are still popular. Families have few appliances; they usually just air-dry clothes after washing and scrape dishes before hand-washing them.

9. In terms of governance, the UK is also remarkable. The unitary state is a very stable constitutional monarchy. Queen Elizabeth II, the current British monarch, has ruled for an amazing sixty-eight years; she is eighty-four years old. The country is also one of only four countries in the world to

have an uncodified constitution. The UK Parliament can perform "constitutional reform" simply by passing Acts. It is wonderful to view the lively debates on the Parliament floor.

10. The UK has fifteen Overseas Territories, former colonies and remnants of the British global empire. It remains a great power, a permanent member of the UN Security Council and other powerful world organizations of power, although no longer of the European Union. At its height, the empire consisted of almost a quarter of the world, the largest empire in world history. Her influence can be observed in the language, culture, legal systems, and governments of many of its former colonies, including still Commonwealth countries like Canada and Australia, the US, India, and even former colonies of the US like my homeland, the Philippines.

That last fact about the Philippine connection clinched it for me. The newlyweds were ready to adopt the country as their own. But it was not meant to be. Her visa application did not work because of a technicality. It turned out that her original visa was unfortunately not convertible to that of an immigrant. They would have had to start the process all over again. That was heartbreaking for them. It was sad for me because I had already fallen in love with the UK but then I love where they eventually settled..

AUSTRALIA, THE NEW A-DREAM

In January 2017, while I was watching the Australian Open on TV in Arizona, I was taken by an ad with a series of scenes and a haunting voice-over by a woman. It was an invitation to see Melbourne's

beauty thru the words of the Aussie poet E. J. Brady in his piece
"Far and Wide:"

> Let me watch the sea rain falling
> Smell the salt, deck-driven spray;
> Let me hear the bush-birds calling
> At the dawning of the day.
>
> Let me see the sun-bars streaming
> Down the valleys, 'ere the night;
> Fills the world with pleasant dreaming
> Love and coolness and delight.

This backdrop for Australia's unique beauty was what floated
in my mind when bushfires raged in Australia, killing wildlife,
destroying many towns, and even enveloping cities with hazardous smoke. They were painful scenes to watch on the nightly TV
news. But then you can just imagine my feelings knowing that
within three months of that tennis open I was watching, I was to
spend four months in this lyrical land, taking care of my newest
grandson.

April and Clint had chosen Melbourne as their new home. And
I was to take care of London-born Kyrie while they settled down in
their new jobs. They were so smart to choose the city. At the time,
it had been named the World's Most Livable City, seven years in a
row. It turns out that their skills and talents, hers as IT program
manager and his as web developer, are ideal for Melbourne which
has top ranking in five factors, the criteria used for determining the
rankings of cities around the world: healthcare, culture and environment, education, infrastructure, and stability.

1. HEALTHCARE

I panicked when my almost two-year-old grandson didn't stop cry-
ing one day. But in just a ten-minute walk, I got him to a clinic. It
was so easy to find a slot for an appointment. Although he wasn't
assigned a permanent doctor, records are well kept so the transfer
of medical information among doctors and staff in the clinic was no
problem. And all care is free. Kyrie was ok; he was just coming on
with a cold.

But the real bedrock of the Australian healthcare system is not
access but prevention through a good quality of life. Work/life balance is held sacred, and companies keep workweeks at forty hours
or under. My son-in-law loves the beer and wine his office serves in
the last couple of hours on Fridays, while my daughter relishes the
chance to see her son early. It's no wonder Australia's average life
expectancy is eighty-two years, #7 in the world (seventy-nine for
the US and seventy-one for the Philippines). This healthy population has navigated the coronavirus pandemic well, ranking #92 in
the world with under 28,000 cases and 900 deaths by the middle of
November 2020.

2. EDUCATION

At the many parties that I attended with friends and relatives who
had also migrated to Melbourne, I got "education" as the answer to
the question "Why is Melbourne the most livable city in the world?"
Elementary and high school education is free. And loans provided to
any student who pursues higher learning come with payment terms
so low and lenient that they might as well be free. A former staffer,
a past colleague, and a grade school classmate all had similar stories.
All their children are already professionals or on the road to becoming one. What a great future my little grandson has.

3. INFRASTRUCTURE

Even if my daughter had not chosen an apartment so centrally located (they now own a home in a suburb), there is an efficient Tram system that takes you anywhere around the city. In fact, it is free to use in the many blocks around the central business district. An additional short bus ride is sometimes necessary, but it was so easy to go to all the places we visited, except for the longer weekend trips when we rented a car. This makes it easy for millennials, like my daughter and son-in-law, to postpone buying a car (they now have one). Road trips are also so much fun because roads are as good and extensive as those in America. As a matter of fact, RVing is as commonplace. And the bridges, both for vehicles and pedestrians, are superb in both form and function.

4. STABILITY

Isolated as a continent, Australia is free from border wars and conflicts. Immigration is largely controlled and strictly based on merit. Even if diversity is high, it is good. The Chinese have recently been coming in droves because they are making large investments in the economy. Rich in natural resources, Australian mining and oil are topped only by services as economic contributors. But what fascinated us most was Australia's wine industry. It is already the fourth largest in the world with more than sixty wine regions. We took road trips to four: Yarra Valley, Mornington Peninsula, the Grampians, and the Pyrenees. And, if you know Bill, that was heaven.

5. CULTURE AND ENVIRONMENT

Many places of interest were within walking distance from their apartment. Frequently, while I was babysitting, Bill would do sight-seeing walks. The South Melbourne Market, just beyond the children's playground, is where Bill and I spent many an afternoon, grandson in tow in his stroller. We relished plates of paella, dubbed the best outside of Spain, oysters, hot jam donuts, borek, dim sims (not dim sum), etc., after buying produce, wine, clothing, or whatever else we needed at home.

In just ten minutes, we could walk in another direction to reach the downtown area. There we hopped on a Yarra River Cruise, explored Comic Con at the Convention Centre, and marveled at modern art in the many galleries. Other times we wandered around Street Art Alleys, relaxed at Federation Square and the Flinders' Station across from it, and shopped at the malls or the fabulous Queen Victoria Market. There were theatres galore, casinos, and good old Chinatown. We caught up on all kinds of reading at the majestic State Library of Victoria with its grand glass ceiling. And sometimes we simply strolled on the Southbank by the river.

A little farther away are lovely parks and gardens. Melbourne Park is where the Australian Open is played. The Royal Botanic, Fitzroy and Carlton Gardens are filled with flowers and plants and the ponds almost hum with ducks, fish, and birds. Museums, shrines, gathering places and other landmarks are located in these green oases right in the middle of the city.

Even refreshing beaches are plentiful nearby—St. Kilda together with the classic Luna Theme Park that is for kids and adults alike; Brighton Beach with its cute and colorful bathing boxes; and Port Melbourne where the ferry to enchanting Tasmania can be boarded. They can all be easily reached by the efficient tram/bus systems.

But it was the road trips during weekends that brought Brady's lyrical poem to life. I saw my first penguins at Philip Island; they are littlest in the world, just a foot tall. We had fruit scones and clotted cream in the refreshing and woodsy mountain town of Sassafras, up in the Dandenong Mountain Range. The Gippsland Lakes National Park was a haven for fishing, crabbing, feasting on seafood, swimming, and photography. But nature was at its best on a tour of The Great Ocean Road where the Twelve Apostles—iconic island pinnacle rocks— still stand.

Australia's "Gold Rush" history came alive in the town of Ballarat on the road to the Grampians National Park, where kangaroos greeted us every morning just outside our B&B door. And at the Healesville Sanctuary we saw koalas, kookaburras, wallabies, wombats, dingos, and Tasmanian devils. But, do you know what made my days on those weekends so bright and cheerful? The wattle trees—the Australian national tree—were all in bloom with yellow flowers everywhere. What more could a girl in love with the color yellow ask for?

My four months in Melbourne showed me why the city deserves the title, "Most Livable City in the World" all those years in a row. It's like the American Dream has been overtaken by a new A-Dream, the Australian Dream. The world surely moves in very mysterious ways. My youngest daughter ended up with the best country for raising a growing family. In fact, she heaves a sigh of relief that coronavirus has hit Australia minimally, while the UK has been hit quite badly. And Bill and I have an awesome new place to visit for more babysitting. I can't wait until a new granddaughter finally comes along. That should give me a few more good months down under.

PART 3
INSIGHTS GAINED

§

"A mind that is stretched by a new experience can
never go back to its old dimensions."

— OLIVER WENDELL HOLMES

This is not strictly a travel quotation. But travel always consists of new experiences, so it is very relevant to us travelers. We are continually open to them and find that our minds do get stretched a lot. They are extended by lessons learned and insights gained. There is a difference between a lesson and an insight. While a lesson teaches us something new, an insight gives us a deeper understanding of what we already know and believe. Lessons help us change to a new version of ourselves. Insights reaffirm us in the process.

Now that we spend six to seven months a year at our Arizona home base at Viewpoint, I have more time to think about our travels. Many times, before I can move on to thinking about what we will do and where we will go next, I tend to muse about the trip just past, relish the fun we just had, and rejoice at insights I just gained from it. Sometimes they are just small thoughts. Other times, they give me a much bigger perspective. The long intervals between our winter and summer trips are a wonderful time to reflect on many concerns of travelers.

By providing me examples, Bill has helped me see more clearly what the best attitude to have while traveling is. He also showed plainly the best ways of dealing with travel mishaps and of handling falling ill while we are on the go. I was also able to articulate that it is curiosity at play in our urge to travel, and that flexibility is a most important trait to develop to handle the changes we encounter while traveling. The time also allowed me to express in a written article my thanks to all the beautiful people I've met on the road.

It was interesting to muse about who are better traveling companions, friends or partners; and to feel blessed that I have both. And, as I appreciated the wonder of the desert spring, I was able to write about what seasons are actually best for travel. In addition, we have stayed long in some places, but sometimes we found that a flash trip was the only thing possible; and so I discussed how much time is best to visit a destination. And I had time to think about what I truly felt about brand new destinations compared to old favorites.

The quality of the transportation infrastructure of a place determines how best to travel there; and it was good to confirm that it is best to travel by road in America and by rail in Europe. I was also finally able to admit that food is so much better at its place of origin, and that is why so many write about the food as part of travel. I even wrote about the courage one has to muster to continue with risky trips that many have warned us about.

Going further, I put in writing how first-time thrills can keep on coming even if sometimes we have to do the same thing over and over again. And after a road trip we did during the pandemic, I was able to frame the evolving rules we followed to be safe, leading to a final chapter on keeping fit on the go. There are many more insights I could write about. I hope that you are entertained by some of the stories that accompany them, and are not just intrigued but also inspired by them.

1

IT'S ALL ABOUT ATTITUDE

Note: This article was originally published in *TravelAwaits*.

Franklin D. Roosevelt once said: "I think we consider too much the good luck of the early bird and not enough the bad luck of the early worm." Yes, certainly luck has two sides to it. And for travelers who constantly put themselves in new places and regularly choose to participate in unfamiliar activities, luck seems to come into play more often than usual. Sometimes a travel day turns out well. Other times it turns out poorly. How do we respond in each situation?

YOU CAN'T CONTROL EVERYTHING

One of the worst days of our life happened in 2018. My husband and I were at Dulles International Airport in Washington D.C. waiting to board a flight bound for London, where we were to catch a connecting flight to Ljubljana, Slovenia. As luck would have it, our airline Primera had declared bankruptcy earlier in the day while we were en route from Phoenix. All its flights had been canceled.

I was terribly upset. Our tickets had been bought at the unbelievably discounted price of $250 per person, but we wound up paying more than ten times that to get to our destination, even after receiving our refund. My husband said, "It's just money." When we arrived in London, he immediately looked for an English pub at the airport. He delighted in a classic English breakfast he had been missing for a while. Bill didn't dwell on the thought that it cost us almost $3,000. He is always unflappable, this Scots-Irish guy.

Don't Be Stymied; Go Ahead

Without hesitation, we went ahead with our travel plans—albeit thousands of dollars poorer. The Slovenia portion of our trip was something we could not postpone. It was dependent on the schedule of our two hosts, whom we had met as tourists in the Philippines a few years earlier. In fact, we had hosted them in the US two years after that meeting.

The centrally located apartments they owned and reserved for us were fully booked for weeks after our agreed schedule. Our room at her bed and breakfast was at the foot of Ljubljana Castle, in front of the huge daily farmers market in Old Ljubljana. In Bled, we got to enjoy his apartment with a balcony overlooking the famous lake and its postcard scenes. We couldn't have asked for more. Our supposed zero-cost week in Slovenia was not just spectacular; it was well worth all of the dollars we had to spend for the replacement tickets.

BE EASY ON YOURSELF: YOU ARE ALLOWED TO MAKE MISTAKES

With the shock of our costly airfare behind us, we proceeded by train to Innsbruck, Austria. From our base there, we decided to take the train to Vienna, stay overnight, then stop in Salzburg, midway on the way back to Innsbruck the next day. At the railway station I got a brochure from the ticket counter while Bill set off to buy a bottle of water. Mixed signals resulted in almost zero time till departure when we finally found each other again. But that got us on the wrong train—the one going in the opposite direction, to Munich.

We had a nonrefundable Airbnb booked in Vienna so we turned around and finally got there at 1:30 pm instead of before lunch as we had planned. I was so stressed. My dear husband said, "Charge it to experience. We're allowed to make mistakes." We made it to St. Stephen's Cathedral, the Mozart House, the opera house, Karlskirche, the Hofburg Palace, and the Museum Quartier. The only Vienna bucket-list site we missed was Schonbrunn Palace.

We'd had to run from place to place but it was great that the landmarks were so close to each other. We even ended the day with dinner complete with sacher torte—a classic Austrian chocolate cake—at a Viennese coffee house. We would've preferred to go to the Hotel Sacher for the original. We were lucky to find out that they have an outlet in Innsbruck.

THERE ARE MANY GOOD PEOPLE ON THE ROAD

Our next base was Oberstaufen, Germany. This is where bad luck started to change into good luck. After one of our long day trips, we missed the shuttle bus back to our resort. Tired and hungry, I must have looked utterly in despair when I found out the next shuttle was an hour and a half away. A German couple who was also waiting at the station proceeded to read each of the posters that were in German, looking for available alternatives for us. They didn't find any, but it didn't matter. It was the friendly effort that counted.

The following day we explored the interesting Hotel Ludwig with many colorful windows on its façade in Steibus, a village close to Oberstaufen. Imagine our surprise when we found the same helpful couple's vacation condo right in front of the RV campground we were visiting adjacent to the hotel. They invited us in for drinks. The awesome thing was that the German man spoke very little English, and my husband spoke very little German. But as women always end up proving, the wife and I did not accept there was an obstacle and ended up gesticulating a lot and understanding each other.

Before we parted, they extended us an invitation to visit them at their home in Uberlinger, Germany. The day before we left for Paris, we found the chance to do just that. On their deck overlooking the legendary Bodensee Lake, we enjoyed a typical German lunch. Then they showed us around the resort city, which was hardly touched during WWII because of various treaties. Meeting such good people is GOOD LUCK in capital letters.

LET THE GOOD TIMES ROLL

By this time we had definitely moved from saying "When it rains, it pours" to "Let the good times roll." In Paris, we were even gifted with a fabulous upgrade from a studio to a one-bedroom apartment. For one romantic week, this elegant home was the base for our day trips to Parisian highlights. The twice-weekly Farmers' Market close by was also heaven-sent, and the outstanding bread pannetone was a most precious find.

In Brussels, Belgium we didn't expect to find one of the most beautiful squares in in all of Europe, the glittering Grand Place that had been designated a UNESCO World Heritage Site since 1998. But food-tripping was another highlight of our stay. We indulged in beef carbonnade, moules frites, beef and cheese fondue, Belgian waffles, Belgian chocolates for me and Belgian beer for Bill. You do have to travel to find the classic original taste of the food we have come to love.

Luck is iffy, especially on the road. We have found that bad luck turns into good luck— sometimes as quickly as it came—and vice versa, of course. What we can control is how we react: to others, to things, and to situations. When bad luck strikes, we should quickly accept the lesson and move on. And when good luck happens, we should let our gratitude freely express itself. This is the kind of attitude that lets the good times really roll.

As a footnote, I also found that people who remain positive whatever kind of luck there is make the best traveling companions. I am so lucky my husband is like that.

2

TRAVEL MISHAPS AND
HOW TO VIEW THEM

§

Travel mishaps are unfortunate accidents, blemishes on the otherwise creamy complexion of an ordinary travel day. I'm not talking about those incidents when we fall ill, but about simple occurrences that we could easily have easily prevented but didn't. And because, as travelers, we are often in unfamiliar places, they seem to happen more when we are on the go. It is therefore important for us to react well when they happen and to learn from them.

TRAPPED IN SNOW

Early in our RVing days, we had to return to our home state for my citizenship interview with the US Citizenship and Immigration Services. We weren't supposed to be in the cold of the north in November, but we had to be. We parked our RV at the Thunderbird RV and Camping Resort in Monroe, Washington. It is riverfront, and there was some fishing to be had. But all of a sudden, a rare snowstorm arrived. It literally buried our RV. We got trapped, and were forced to cancel our traditional Thanksgiving dinner. That was ok, but I also had to skip my birthday night out.

We had very little propane left, our lone energy source for the heater and stove. So we confined ourselves to microwaveable dishes. Management could not risk their pipes freezing, so we also were forced to scrimp on the little water we had left in the fresh water tank. Fortunately, even with TV and Wifi available, we relished the opportunities it gave us for non-routine ways of interacting. Bill acted the boy scout, venturing to hike through the snow for errands. But what he loved best was that I just simply followed his instructions. It was a situation I was totally unfamiliar with, and it turned out to be a welcome change.

FLAT RV TIRES

Later, however, we had a scarier RV mishap. Driving down Interstate 71 from Cincinnati, Ohio to Louisville, Kentucky, the right front tire of the RV blew out. There were eight tires in all, two in front, two in the middle, and four at the rear on two axles. It was such a loud noise, strange to my ears. I got scared. But Bill was able to steer our 20,000-pound rig off the road even though there was very little space available, right on the edge where the guard rails met the overpass ahead.

He remained calm and called Good Sam. Then he got the Rummikub game out and played a few games with me, even tactically letting me win, while we waited inside the RV on that hot afternoon without air conditioning. After what seemed like a long time, help arrived and the tire was replaced. The rescue truck accompanied us all the way to Louisville, because the mechanic said a lot of our tires needed changing. It was midnight when we arrived at their shop. We were both tired but, as usual, my husband was that good old boy scout I had married.

GETTING LOST

And that is why, in Helsinki, I panicked when I thought I lost him. After a failed hostel experiment in Oslo, we chose Hotel Ava, a very affordable lodging option because it was part of a Hotel Management Institute that provided most of the staff. The only problem was it was twenty minutes away from the city center. We solved that with a Helsinki card that not only paid for all of the museums and cruises, but also for all the public transportation. We loved the hotel. It was as if we were going "home" every day after our tours.

On our last day, when we had finished our packing, we went for a last walk around the neighborhood. We found an old church, a nice neighborhood, and an antique shop of interest. The people were so warm that every time we looked at a map, someone would approach us and ask what we were looking for. The streets had double signs, in Finnish and Swedish, but there were none in English. It was good everyone was eager to help though. When we got back, we stashed our bags in the lobby, ready for the 3 pm public bus that would take us to the airport. Having more than thirty minutes left to wait, Bill went to the pharmacy we'd seen just around the corner, having forgotten to buy something.

I waited, and waited, and waited. By 2:45 pm, I was already in panic mode. He had not come back. I berated the receptionist for not giving him a map. Then I cried. I imagined all sorts of things that could have happened to him. At five minutes before 3 pm, he walked in, a bit flustered. He quickly instructed me to follow him to the bus stop. I ran all the way, lugging my carry-on through the cobbled streets, unmindful if it got damaged. He said, "They are just mishaps, not tragedies. They are just opportunities to try to be smarter the next time." He'd again showed me by example how to stay calm, cool, and collected.

3

Falling Ill When You Least Expect It

§

The most unfortunate thing that can happen when you are traveling is to get sick in the middle of all the excitement of your trip. In our twelve years of traveling together, I remember four times when something like that happened to us. Once every three years may not be that bad; but, let me tell you, it was very bad each time one happened.

The Flu in Iceland

The first was during a cruise called the Enrichment Voyage on the MV Explorer, the two weeks to one month when adults are allowed to join their Semester at Sea program. This is the unique cruise that allows college students to earn credits on board a cruise ship when country experiences are at the heart of the degree programs of their choice. The route took us to Copenhagen, Denmark, three cities in Iceland, the Shetland Islands of Scotland, Belfast, Ireland, and finally, our disembarkation port, Southampton, England. Whenever we were at sea, the professors who were on board held enrichment courses for us on topics like the economy, culture, and geography of the country we were about to see.

Before we embarked in Stockholm, Sweden, we had just finished a tour of Oslo, Norway, Helsinki, Finland, and Russia. You can imagine how much excitement was building up. Unfortunately, it also meant that we were not fresh for travel. So, right after our tour of Reykjavik, we both fell ill, had chills, fever, colds, and cough en route to the small fishing town of Isofjodur in western Iceland. Bill still braved the excursion to the remote town. I couldn't, and had to be content with a short photo session from the deck, all bundled up.

By then, the small clinic on the ship had become as busy as the buffet stations on the upper decks. Dozens of our shipmates had fallen ill, too. We concluded that some virus was going around. By the time we reached Akureyri in northern Iceland, I was well enough to join the tours. We are happy that it was only the usual flu virus and not the novel coronavirus of today. We now think it's not a good idea to join a ship that has been cruising for a year, even if it is heavily discounted. Just like the current experience with Covid, those young students might not have been showing symptoms even if they were infected since their immune systems were much better than ours. It did not help that we had just come from an exhausting Baltic tour.

CARDIOVASCULAR PROBLEMS

The second occasion happened in the first week of December 2011; but I have already told that story in detail. So, let me turn to the third instance. It happened in 2013 when we made a long road trip to visit our children in Idaho, Alberta, Washington, and Colorado. Visiting family is always exciting, the kind of travel I always look forward to because I am able to see some sights while cooking for them and spoiling the grandkids. We left the RV in storage in Mesa, Arizona and drove to Idaho, then Alberta, Canada. On the way back, Bill drove for twelve hours in one day from Calgary to Seattle. Just two days later, he drove for nineteen hours in two days to Colorado.

In Denver, Bill felt a painful knot behind his left knee. By the third day, his whole left leg, from the hip to his foot, was feeling numb, tight, and painful. We went to the urgent care center and were quickly dispatched to the emergency room of the nearest hospital. What we feared had happened. They found several blood clots in his left leg. After more blood tests, he was given injections to break down the clots and tablets to thin out his blood.

We were not allowed to drive to Mesa, Arizona until his INR (international numerical ratio) was 2.5 to 3.5. This took a week. In the meantime, I again had a flare-up of hives, although milder this time. After this incident, we agreed to set six hours as our maximum driving time in a day. We also agreed to make sure we had a good solid rest stop after the first three hours.

It is good the two cardiovascular problems happened in America, where we are entitled to Medicare. Just imagine how scary and costly it would have been if they had happened where the healthcare systems were foreign to us, where we don't know anybody who could help us, and where Medicare is not available and we had to pay for every procedure? It would then be more terrifying.

A MACULAR HOLE

The third instance happened just last year. While I was on our usual summer road trip, during mass in Calgary, I noticed that when I closed my left eye, the priest seemed so far away. It was scary. When I tried to read the words of the gospel songs projected on the screen, the letters were all distorted. That was scarier. I called my eye doctor in Phoenix, Arizona but the nurse practitioner said that the doctor was not available for two weeks and warned that if I saw flashes of light, I should go to an emergency room right away. That was scariest.

When we got back to Phoenix the doctor immediately referred me to a retinal specialist. His diagnosis: a full-thickness (Stage III) macular hole in my right eye (the macula is the part of the retina responsible for detailed central vision). He ordered a vitrectomy and membrane peel, a delicate surgery that involves the suctioning of the vitreous fluid from the eye, repairing the hole with tiny instrumentation, and placing a gas bubble to allow the hole to close and heal, and the fluid to refill the eye.

There was only one catch. The four-month recovery period included total face-down positioning for the first to second weeks, the key to keeping the hole closed. Anyone who knows me would have said that was an impossible task for this Queen of Impatience. It is good that a company now rents out a Vitrectomy Support Equipment, a chair that allows face-down positioning to be bearable, even somewhat comfortable, seated—or when taken apart, lying down.

Bill was a great caregiver but the boredom nearly killed me because I could not read well at all. After six weeks, when no further improvement in vision was expected, my optometrist took measurements for new glasses. I had read that patients usually improve to 20/40 but sometimes end up with 20/50 (20/20 is best). My bad luck is that I got stuck at 20/60. The repair had unluckily left more scarring than expected. The distortion could not be improved.

Our diet is now focused on eye health. I had eliminated eggs after my husband's cardiovascular problems, but I brought them back because they are great for our eyes. Anyway, he also suffers from macular degeneration. I have doubled our intake of fruits and vegetables, reducing meats at the same time. Fruits and vegetables are rich in lutein and zeaxanthin, antioxidants needed by the macula. Also important are foods like walnuts, wild-caught fish, and other foods rich in Omega-3 fatty acids.

With health issues becoming more serious as we age, there are only two things my husband and I think we can do if we want to continue traveling. One, keep ourselves as healthy as we can; and two, make sure that our travels err on the side of utmost comfort and convenience, despite the cost. Falling ill while you are on the go can be tragic. Instead of having fun, we are constrained by that possibility. And the consequences may be even direr than that.

4

YOU CAN RELIVE FIRST TIME THRILLS

§

Lady Bird Johnson once said: "When I no longer thrill to the first snow of the season, then I'll know I am growing old."

We almost never have snow in the desert. I said, almost. At our New Year's Eve Party somewhere north of Phoenix, snow snippets suddenly fell one year. It was a first-time thrill of undeniably huge proportions. People who live in places where snow is a winter's staple still regularly feel it during the first snow of the season. But the thrill we felt might take forever before it wears off.

I refuse to grow old. But I do not think it is age that really matters to experience thrills like that. I don't even think it is the place. I think what matters most is one's attitude, how much one wants to experience thrills again and again. It is all a matter of being wide-eyed, curious, and yes, refusing to grow old. And it is a matter of traveling more, because that ensures that such first-time thrills can happen much more frequently as you roam unfamiliar, enchanted roads.

FLYING A KITE

Even before we went RVing, I'd experienced a wild euphoric moment. I was finally able to do the one thing I had never been able to do throughout my childhood. We had traveled to visit my sister in Falls Church, Virginia. Down at windy Virginia Beach, my husband mustered all the patience in the world to help me experience flying my first-ever kite.

We were, in fact, so preoccupied that there was no photo taken of that precious moment. Nevertheless, when we chanced upon the World Kite Museum at Long Beach, Washington the following year, I felt more entitled to enjoy the place. Unfortunately, however, I am still struggling to find ways to learn how to ride a bike. Many have tried to teach me; many have failed.

PLUNGING INTO WATER

Two years later, I experienced the first-time thrill again at the World Waterpark inside the world's fourth-largest shopping center, the West Edmonton Mall in Edmonton, Alberta, Canada. There was an intermediate water slide called the Corkscrew which had two completely enclosed slides that twist, turn, and drop into a 1.2-meter-deep pool. You see, I can't swim. As a matter of fact, I am able to wade only in three-feet-deep water where I feel safe enough to play. My very supportive husband promised he would be at the end of the big pipe, ready to rescue me from any mishap.

That's all I needed. As I cascaded down, I was still deathly afraid, especially when it got so dark, I felt so alone, and didn't know if I was about to meet my Maker and drown in the pool. But when I came out of that long, dark pipe, my husband was right there waiting for me. He immediately cuddled me in his arms, saying: "See how easy and fun it is?" I was all smiles and thanked him profusely for helping me get another "first-time trophy" and for always being my hero. Admittedly, he is the also the main reason I can travel and collect more first time thrills.

RVING TO THE ARCTIC CIRCLE

I know I have told you a bit about this story but let me tell it to you now in more detail here. Somebody once said, "If it excites you and scares you at the same time, then it probably means you should do it." That's exactly how I felt when we drove our RV over Dempster Highway to the Arctic Circle in Canada's Yukon. We actually passed up the first opportunity to do so from Fairbanks, Alaska on the shorter and better Dalton Highway. It just so happened that I had waited all night for the Northern Lights to appear in Dawson City. Extremely disappointed, I was fiercely determined to look for another thrill.

How could my husband have refused? Excited at the prospect of going as far north as we possibly could, we also felt scared that our old Class B motorhome would not withstand the rigors of the road, and that there would be no one to help us in such a deserted place in case we ran into trouble. It truly was a muddy dirt gravel road that we had to drive on for four days round trip. That fear may have added to the drama and the thrill.

But all those worries were soon forgotten when we witnessed the unique fall spectacle of the alpine tundra. First, it was the trees and shrubs becoming increasingly shorter but continuing to be bright red, orange, and gold. Then, around the Tombstone Territorial Park, the scenery became an autumnal carpet of lichens, fungi, and small plants that hugged the landscape. Finally, we had the scene we wanted, shivering in that quiet windy deserted spot very far north.

OTHER FIRST-TIME THRILLS

I could write about other times like when I saw my first bison in Yellowstone, the first bear in Yosemite, or my first alligator in the Everglades. How about seeing, for the first time, the radiantly yellow wattle trees in bloom in Australia? When I got on the helicopter to see the inaccessible sights around Kauai, or that small plane that got me close enough to see the spectacle of Mt. Everest, my heart fluttered at first and then I felt giddy.

There have been many other firsts, and there will be many more. I still have not been able to ride a hot-air balloon, appreciate the Great Barrier Reef up close and personal, or see those bigger penguins in the wild in faraway Antarctica. However, as a certain Steven White once said: "If at first you don't succeed, then skydiving definitely isn't for you." I will, therefore, exclude skydiving from my pursuit of first-time thrills until the day I die. But, yes, I will keep traveling as long as Bill is willing and able to support this passion of ours.

5

YOU MUST GET USED TO CHANGE

§

It has often been said that, if there's anything constant in this world, it is change. And may I add that, when you are on the go, like we travelers almost always are, change happens at an even faster rate. We must get used to it; in fact, we must expect it; and we must be prepared for it. In other words, we have to be flexible and adaptable.

A CONGESTED CITY

I remember the folly of resisting local ways. During our 2009 three-week tour of Mexico, we parked our RV in Teotihuacan, where the most visited pre-Hispanic ruins of the oldest civilization in North America are located, approximately twenty-five miles northeast from Mexico City. On a day trip to Ciudad de Mexico, we took the public bus. With a population of eighteen million, it is one of the most congested cities in the world—much like Metro Manila where I grew up.

We loved our tour of Catedral Metropolitana, Templo Mayor, Plaza de la Constitucion, Palacio Nacional, and the shopping at Avenida Central. We ended our day with a visit of Chapultepec Castle. It was already night time when we finished with what we wanted to see. We should have known that it was going home time for millions of workers in Mexico City. With a sea of humanity looking to ride the train, there were more people than capacity. The men were being segregated from women in separate carriages to prevent chances of unwanted close encounters. I was horrified.

I didn't want to be separated from Bill so we hailed a taxi instead. In the ensuing confusion, Bill not only lost his cellphone but we also lost a lot of money and time on the taxi ride through the traffic-congested city. Good thing we still made it to the last bus to Teotihuacan. I am a serious planner, but plans didn't work that time. We should have gone home an hour earlier or boarded in separate carriages. I didn't adapt.

A SHOWER AT THE SINK

Nothing illustrates this more than the embarrassingly awkward and funny incident I had to endure in Chicken, Alaska. I may have mentioned this in an earlier chapter but I tell it here in greater detail. We had only been RVing for several months. After having spent and enjoyed a cool summer month in Alaska, we decided to go back to the Lower 48 on a different route, north through Chicken, Alaska. The road there was all gravel. At the time, the town's population was thirty-two which regularly dwindles to seven at wintertime.

Taking a shower in this little town proved highly challenging for me. I had enough loonies—Canadian coins— for maybe a five-minute hot shower at the RV campground. But I ended up having to rinse at the sink in a room with no heater. I complained to my husband, "The instructions were not clear!" He told me I was supposed to put in an additional loonie before each time segment ran out, not all at once at the beginning. I did not finish my shower well and it was good that it was still early fall; it wasn't that cold yet.

Some showers do not have outlets for blow dryers; some do not have mirrors; some only have hot water, and the way to mix hot and cold water was different every time; so with the specific way to pay. I learned only too well, and pretty fast thereafter; that flexibility and adaptability is a virtue one must cultivate, because every few days we were in a new "home."

A Failed Long Layover

I went to Australia to babysit my youngest grandson in Melbourne, where my daughter and her husband had migrated. Cheapskate that I was, I opted for the lowest fares, which had long layovers in Guangzhou, China. I foolishly thought that the long layovers would be chances for touring the second largest city of China (Shanghai is the first). On the way there, I found out that the seven-hour layover wasn't long enough to allow a city tour. Travel time would already be four hours. I decided to try on the way back when I would have twelve hours.

So I spent those seven hours in the Baiyun International Airport of Guangzhou. I hunkered down to get lost in my social media world. Sadly, with my laptop charge down to zero, I spent most of my time finding out how I could power it up with the gadgets thrown into my computer bag by my loving husband. But with a mechanical aptitude of near zero, I was ultimately unsuccessful. Luckily, my perfect husband had also thrown in a portable battery for my phone.

The power problem solved, I next looked for signs that indicated free airport WiFi. When I found it, I could not get my phone to connect. A couple of Chinese millennials finally took pity and showed me how. With about half of my layover time already wasted, I thought I would at least have some fun time on my phone. But I should have remembered that Facebook is banned in China. I turned to surfing on the Net, but I was equally floored. Every search pointed me to sites totally foreign, totally unfamiliar, and totally Chinese. My isolation was complete. I should have brought a book. I was totally unprepared for this. Just imagine what would happen during my twelve-hour layover on the way back if, again, I am not able to go on a city tour.

It is hard to make a seventy-year-old woman become more flexible. But I love to travel, so I would have to keep on trying. There's no giving up here. I know that anything can be handled with better preparation and some prior knowledge. But, in the absence of both, a hefty dose of good attitude, specifically of flexibility or adaptability, is all that is needed. For example, I should have looked for a Chinese-translation site and learned some Chinese in four hours. Ha!

6

BEAUTIFUL PEOPLE
ON THE ROAD

§

A nd I'm not talking about beauty contest winners, glamorous celebrities, or as-yet undiscovered nymphs. My definition of "beautiful" in this post is this: "of a very high standard; excellent." As travelers, we get exposed to many unfamiliar, uncomfortable, even unnerving situations. During such trying times, when you meet people whom you don't even know but who step up to help with actions of the highest order, consider yourself lucky. You have just been privileged to meet a beautiful person.

A BEAUTIFUL TAIWANESE
Nine years ago, Bill and I had just gotten married and we flew to the Philippines to introduce my home country to my groom. On the way back, we stopped at Taipei, Taiwan to visit his expat friend for a couple of weeks. The small country island was easy to visit

with a High-Speed Rail System that can take you from Taipei, the capital in the north, to Kaohsiung, the southernmost urban center in just two and a half hours. One of our day trips using the system was to Tainan, the old capital, in the southwest.

Taiwan's capital for 200 years during the Koxinga and Qing dynasties, Tainan boasts of many old fortresses, historic temples, and rich folk cultures. After visiting Fort Provintia, the Dutch fortress, and the oldest Confucian Temple of Taiwan, we took the bus to the Taiwan Salt Museum in the Qigu suburban district. The bus driver did not speak a word of English but took pains to help us understand that we'd better be on the same spot where he let us off at 3 pm for the last bus back to Tainan.

The Museum consists of a huge salt mountain, salt spas, and the building housing the exhibits, built on the site of what was once the country's largest sea salt field before the salt mines ceased operations in 2002. As luck would have it, we missed the bus. After anxious moments with the non-English-speaking staff, the Manager came and ordered a taxi for us. It came an hour later, by which time I was already very hungry. We could only find a cup of coffee for Bill. Inside the cab, the driver noticed my fidgeting. I must have looked so hungry because he stopped the cab, got out, opened the trunk, and handed me a package of the best crackers I have ever tasted.

BEAUTIFUL MEXICANS

From Nogales, Arizona on our RV trip through Mexico, our first stop was Hermosillo, Mexico. Our RV Park was right along the highway; it was easy to find. It was quite unnerving, however, that we were the lone RV in the park. The next night, we had a more difficult time looking for our next campground. We stopped at a gas station to fill up and, in broken Spanish, asked about where the Los Mochis Trailer Park could be. Two rough looking young men in a beat-up car in front of us looked at the address I had scribbled on a piece of paper and quickly motioned us to follow them.

The next ten minutes were truly uneasy ones. But the two men did lead us to Hotel Los Mochis; our RV Park was the hotel's back parking lot. We offered some pesos for their help; but the young men graciously refused our gesture. That night we may have been again the lone RV in the trailer park but no fear settled in. We had just met two beautiful Mexicans.

The next day we met more. We wanted to buy some groceries at Ley, a Mexican grocery chain. When we were about to enter the parking lot, a stray grocery cart was left right in the middle of the road by the usual uncaring busy shoppers. Well, the driver of the car just exiting the lot stopped, got out, and moved the cart away so we could pass. Beautiful people are all over Mexico. And that is one reason we have adopted it as our third home.

A Beautiful Family in the UK

In 2014 we were on a UK road trip on the way to my youngest daughter's wedding at the Guthrie Castle in Scotland. I was with my eldest daughter, her daughter, and Bill. The road trip was to take us from London to Stonehenge, Bath, the Cotswolds, Wales, and back to Windsor Castle and London before the flight to Edinburgh. With plenty of sight-seeing planned, our hotel stays were going to be just sleeping time. Our first night was at the Farmers Hotel, between Stonehenge and Bath in the town of Warminster.

The building was 300 years old. It was difficult getting our luggage up the narrow, convoluted stairway. But the beds were comfy. Famished, we quickly went down to the Italian Restaurant on the premises for dinner. Our pasta and pizza dinner was delicious, but that was not what we will remember from this hotel. It was the company that was remarkable.

It was run by a small Italian family. The father was the Manager, his three sons the Chef, waiter and butler, and his daughter, the cashier. That evening our families became one. The Chef was so happy he gave us tons of free dessert and the father invited us to watch the World Cup Championships on the big TV after dinner. Although England lost, it was such a fun night. My granddaughter got up early the next day to buy a potted plant as a gift to the family. Lots of souvenir photos were taken before we headed out for Bath.

Luxurious facilities, excellent locations, and wonderful amenities may make the most popular lodging features, but places like the Farmers Hotel are one in a million. My daughter thanked me profusely for selecting the hotel. Today we both still keep in touch with the Italian family's daughter through Facebook. This small Warminster family, the three Mexicans, and the Chinese taxi driver are some of the most beautiful people we have ever met on the road.

7

Traveling with Friends or with Your Partner

§

The only section of Asia that lies partly within the Southern Hemisphere is the region called Southeast Asia. My home country the Philippines is part of it. Many view the region as exotic because of its varied and distinctive cultures. Chinese and/or Malay ethnicities are mixed with western influences from shared histories of subjugation by foreign colonizers, such as the Portuguese, Spanish, Dutch, French, British, and Americans.

In this part of the world you will encounter colorful native costumes, graceful exotic dances, ornate temples and historical churches, white beaches with vestiges of WWII, world-class diving destinations, undulating rice terraces, and perfect volcanic cones. String them together in one unforgettable getaway and you will find that those same shared histories produce unbelievable warmth in its peoples. It is a foundation for fun in the Orient.

My husband is most interested in traveling to this intriguing part of the world, but that was not enough for him to join me in a tour of Malaysia, Laos, Thailand, and Brunei in September 2017. It was understandable. I was supposed to be in Manila for business and thus only for a short time. Still, I used the opportunity to steal a few days to take the trip with three of my long-time girlfriends. But even I must admit that four days in four countries is too fast. After the trip, I realized how traveling with girlfriends is very different from traveling with a partner.

DIFFERENCE #1: FAST VS. SLOW TRAVEL.

Fast travel fits in as many sights, cities, even countries into one trip as possible. You give a quick look and simply plan to return to the place you could not get enough of later. On the other hand, slow travel means taking the time to explore each destination to get a better appreciation of the local culture. My husband thinks it's insane to see only a little bit of many different areas rather than to get to know one small area well. My girlfriends and I, on the other hand, can be satisfied with getting our photos taken at famous landmarks and then, *voila*, next!

On our four-day trip we started with an overnight layover in Malaysia, stayed at the airport hotel, and arrived in Laos the following day. We had time and opportunity for the one most important thing to do: have the famous Hainanese chicken rice from the most popular chain. Fortunately, there was a busy branch in the airport's Food Court.

In Vientiane, the Laotian capital, we had a day and a half targeting the top six attractions: the Buddha Park of 200 statues of the religious leader, the majestic Golden Stupa, the Patuxai Victory Monument (Asia's Arc de Triomphe), the Presidential Palace, and two other Wats (temples). Our visit was capped with a Laotian mass at a Catholic Church.

Then we had another overnight layover in Bangkok, staying at the airport hotel. A Wat just around the corner was typical, and we witnessed a funeral there. But, not satisfied with that, we hired a car to take us to downtown Bangkok. We not only got the chance to feast on delicious Thai seafood but had the awesome opportunity to get night views of the Grand Palace, the city's iconic wats, and the home of the father of the King. We capped the thrill-filled night with shopping at the city's largest night market. Dozens of lovely US $1 scarves found their way into our luggage.

The next day we were ready for our day and a half in Brunei. You may not believe it, but we were able to visit eight of its top attractions: three different types of mosques, the Water Village, the Royal Regalia Museum, the sprawling Official Residence of the Sultan, his modest boyhood home, and the six-star (sic) Empire Resort and Country Club. We were very impressed. The nation is a bastion of understated elegance and luxury.

DIFFERENCE #2: SHOPPING TIME AND STYLE

This is the opposite of #1. Women take their time to shop. We scour an area for different outlets to survey the available local supply of all things possible, and then take the time at chosen shops before selecting something. And when we have zeroed in on something we just have to have, we love bargaining for a better value sometimes, or most of the time, just for the sake of bargaining. Men, on the other hand, don't have the patience to do this and would rather wait for us at a café, read a newspaper or book, and drink a latte. When they themselves look for something, they go to the few places they trust. Then, they may not even care enough about the price.

At the Malaysian airport we shopped for souvenir items. In Laos we were able to squeeze in a trip to a Night Market near our Ibis Vientiane Hotel. We made it to the Chatuchak Night Market in downtown Bangkok. And in Brunei, we happily got stuck in the shopping mall when heavy rain poured. I am sure my husband would have gone shopping with me to all these; he is more patient than most men. Girlfriends, however, invariably find something, and then the others say, "I gotta have that too!" Or there is a blunt, honest answer when I ask, "Does this look good on me?" Shopping with girlfriends is thus more synergistic. And that is probably why we all end up buying more than what we initially plan.

SIMILARITY #1: LOVE OF CULTURE, HISTORY, AND LANDMARKS

The love of exploring local culture, history, and landmarks is shared by men and women. There may be some little differences. My husband would also have gone to all the attractions we went to, the only difference being that he would have taken a couple more days to do it. And he probably would spend more time exploring war memorials or playing in the water more than me, the former because he is a man and the latter because I can't swim. The final difference is that he would probably spend a whole lot less time taking photos, if any.

SIMILARITY #2: DINING

The other major similarity is the love of good food. He would have loved doing what we did in Laos. We spent big bucks to savor a Laotian meal at a five-star hotel. He would have loved what we did in Brunei, too. We again splurged on a full course lunch at the six-star—no, I didn't make a mistake—Empire Resort Hotel. And, oh, he might have paid for all of them, too.

I am truly blessed that I can enjoy both kinds of travel. My girlfriends are ready, willing, and able to travel with me. And then there is my loving husband who is always close by. He has even orchestrated our next phase of slower travel for over a month in Europe at one week per country; and an even slower travel of three months a year at all-inclusive resorts in Mexico. Don't you think I am one lucky lady, still cruising both ways, past seventy?

8

WHICH SEASON IS THE BEST TIME TO TRAVEL

§

When fall comes, mainstream and social media gets flooded with pictures and videos of trees and shrubs that have turned red, orange, yellow, and gold. You are probably all saying your ooohs and aaahs, whether you are where you can see them in person or not. Sometimes I wish I could live in such a place, if only I don't have to face the cold drab winter that comes after.

THE CASE FOR FALL

Fall used to be my favorite season of all, hands down. I remember the maple tree I had behind my townhome in Seattle. A deciduous tree common in the North, the leaves turn bright yellow, orange, scarlet or maroon. I love those trees whose leaves become different colors, but individual trees with single-hued leaves can also be dazzling especially if they stand beside trees of contrasting colors. The sugar maple is the best one of all. As the months pass, it makes a complete color wheel, first in several shades of green, then turning from yellow to orange, and finally, red. Sadly, as is meant to be, the changing of colors signify that the leaves are in the process of dying. When winter comes, they fall.

Farther north of the Northern Hemisphere, fall foliage is completely yellow. Aspens, a regular feature in those areas, growing in high-altitude areas such as mountains or high plains, turn monochromatic; they turn yellow. That is I why I love fall in Alaska and the Rockies. I am a true xanthophile, a lover of the brightness of the color yellow.

THE CASE FOR SPRING

When we settled in the Phoenix area I thought I would only be seeing drab earth colors. That was, until I saw the wildflowers that painted the desert floor in the whole rainbow spectrum when springtime comes. As beautiful as that picture sounds, that is not what really gave me the best surprise of all. I reasoned that I still prefer fall in the Northeast because the color swatches are larger since they are splashed on to big trees and in wide stretches of them. Well------imagine my extreme delight when I saw that the desert trees called paloverdes—meaning green wood or stick in Spanish—which are green most of the year, sprout little yellow blossoms when springtime comes. In fact, at their peak, they cover almost the entire crown, and the whole tree, in effect, becomes sunshiny yellow.

There are two varieties of paloverdes, and they bloom at separate times, so the golden blaze stays around for at most two months, from mid-March to mid-May, in a good year. The Foothill paloverde has more yellowish bark and true yellow flowers. Blue paloverdes, on the other hand, have twigs, young branches, and leaves that are bluish-green, and flowers that are bordering on orange. In our neck of the woods, both species are everywhere: parking places, freeway banks, public and private gardens, other public places, and in all kinds of parks.

The first to bloom are the Blue paloverdes, with the Foothills following about two to three weeks later. Their flowers both have five petals, with the banner petal standing out above the plane of the other four. In Blues, the banner petal is yellow, sometimes with orange spots. The Foothills' banner petal is white. Once these flowers are pollinated, they produce edible beans.

And that is the big difference between spring and fall. Spring signals the beginning of new life; the flowers turn into food. Fall, in turn, signals the end; the leaves fall and the tree sleeps. I think I now love desert spring more. It's as if the sun unloads its energy, leaves its rays on everything it touches, the color yellow gets trapped in the flowers, and the whole scene radiates the sunshine back to the universe. So I make it a point to be home from my travels in April.

And so my favorite place and time to travel should be blazing fall, which is a great shoulder season for bargain travel to many places, to witness the colors of this season in other places. Since it is too cold in the desert in winter and too hot in summer, you will find us traveling in late fall and throughout winter, making sure we are home by April. And, of course, we are also gone during the height of summer, when it sizzles in the dessert, to go to cooler places. In turn, I invite everyone to come to the desert in spring. You will be amazed. And it will be cool, both literally and figuratively.

9

ARE A FEW HOURS ENOUGH?

§

Time is the kind of commodity which, when we lose it, we cannot get a morsel back. So I usually pack a lot into whatever time is available at the places we visit. When we were in Innsbruck, for example, we felt we had to visit the great cities of Vienna and Salzburg, too. The latter is two hours east from Innsbruck and Vienna is two hours further east from Salzburg.

The solution was simple. Leave Innsbruck by 7:30 am, arrive in Vienna by 11:30 am, retire in a Viennese apartment by 6:30 pm, leave for Salzburg at 8 am in the morning, arrive at 10 am, start back to Innsbruck at 5 pm, and arrive at 7 pm. That would give us seven hours of sightseeing in Vienna and seven hours in Salzburg, too. Or so we thought.

THE CASE OF VIENNA

What was supposed to be a brilliant solution proved troublesome for these newbies in Austria. I have told you about the time we lost each other in the Innsbruck Hauptbahnhof (Main Railway Station), and found each other almost two hours later, when the conductor who checked our ticket, told us that we were on the train to Munich, in the wrong direction.

It was already 1:30 pm when we got to Vienna. We still covered quite a few landmarks but, because the city is the biggest in Austria with 2.6 million in population, we were rushing from one to the other, walking fast and hurriedly taking photos. It was not the way to enjoy that lovely city. Our visit time was reduced from a planned seven to an actual five.

Still, we saw the grandness of St. Stephen's Cathedral and witnessed the buzz at StephenPlatz, which even had public Wifi and modern electric cars that shuttled tourists around. Just around the corner was the Mozart Haus but, of course, we didn't have time to go into the museum. Then we walked to the Vienna State Opera House, passing by the long lines at the Café Sacher that originated the famous sacher torte. Alas, we didn't have time to taste the legendary dessert. At the Opera House we spent some time looking at the plaza stars dedicated to great composers who had performed there.

We continued walking to the KarlsKirche, a domed cathedral with a huge viewing platform and fountain. Hungry, we sampled the ubiquitous puffers being roasted and sold by vendors on the sidewalks, along with chestnuts and potato slices. But again, we didn't have the chance to go inside the church; there was a queue at the ticket booth. On the way to the Hofburg Palace, we chanced upon the Secession Building, an exhibition hall built in 1897 as an architectural manifesto for a group of rebel artists seceding from the long-established fine art institution. The Palace, on the other hand, had become the national library. We didn't get the chance to go inside. Across from it is the Museum Quartier which is akin to the Smithsonian Institution in America. We barely got to appreciate it except for a few photos. But I loved taking a photo of the classic tourist trolley we chanced upon in front of the beautiful architecture of old buildings for a beautiful memento.

And across from the Quartier we found Café Raymond where we had a quick dinner, some wine, and finally a slice of sacher torte—albeit not the original. Our apartment was only four stops away on the subway. We slept well but felt quite disappointed. We may have seen eight Viennese landmarks, but we really did not get to know the city that is considered to be in the Top Ten of the Most Livable Cities in the world.

THE CASE OF SALZBURG

In Salzburg, we had the seven hours we had planned. And Salzburg is a lot smaller with a population of 150,000. From the Hauptbahnhof we simply walked to the Mirabell Palace on the way to the Old Town Square. The Palace and Garden are where Maria—played by Julie Andrews in the movie "The Sound of Music"— together with the von Trapp children sang the classic song "Do Re Mi". We wasted much time here, with me trying to look and sound like Maria—an exercise in futility. Salzburg is the city where most of "The Sound of Music" was filmed. That alone gave a spring to our steps.

On the way out, we chanced upon a farmer's market across the street. How much luckier could we have been? We were told that it is staged every Thursday. We found it a haven for local food, produce, plants, and even dry goods. We sort of got stuck there and did not leave until Bill had enjoyed a farmer's version of the famous apple strudel, and I had bought a fifteen euro leather purse. We could have stayed more hours because there were tents where a lot of alcoholic drinks and other goodies were being sampled for free, but we had to move on. We told ourselves we had to be back in Innsbruck before nightfall.

Right before reaching the Old Town Square, we noticed a gleaming bridge. When we got closer, we realized it was glistening because of the way the sun was hitting the many locks left there by couples in love. Because of its location, it was the best such bridge we had seen from all over the world. After the bridge, we looked for the place where Mozart was born at #9 Getreidegasse. Although the street had become a shopping mecca, the Mozart Haus still dominated the scene. Unfortunately, we didn't have time to visit it.

Just about a block away is the historic center of Salzburg called Residence Platz, a large, stately square named after the Residential building of the Prince-Archbishop of Salzburg. In front of the building, beside the Cathedral and in the middle of the Square, is the beautiful Residenzbrunnen, the fountain which is another famous point in "The Sound of Music" Tour. Seeing these places evoked even more of the feel-good emotions watching the movie gave us.

The Square defined by the Salzburg Cathedral—which still contains the baptismal font used for Mozart— together with St. Peter's Abbey and the Residential Building is called the Dom Platz, where carriages can be hired for tours. When we were there, a newly-wed couple was very happily parading in one. From that Square, you can see the Salzburg Fortress up the hill; you can also get a glimpse of it from Mirabell.

When it was time for an Austrian early dinner, we walked past the Residenzbrunnen Fountain to the Visitors Information Center at Mozart Platz—where a large statue of Mozart stands—to ask for recommendations. They pointed us to Swelter's, where Bill and I had *wienerschnitzel* and *griesnockerlsuppe*. It was a great meal that capped a day with great memories of "The Sound of Music, Austrian cuisine—both fine dining and street food— music, Mozart, and the love bridge. Yes, we got to know Salzburg in just seven hours. The Salzburg allure is truly hard to miss, even if you only have a short time.

You will have a fifty-fifty chance of knowing and enjoying a city even if you have little time. Remember, though, that the bigger the city, the more time you should reserve for it, especially if it is such a culturally significant city as Vienna. But we didn't regret our visit there. In general, since we may not pass a particular way again, we should always take the chance to visit a place even if you do not have enough time. In other words, it is better to see part of it than nothing at all.

10

Brand New or Old Favorite?

§

B ack in the day, I would choose a brand new destination every single time. When I retired and started this traveling saga, it had been all about learning something new, doing something different, and seeing an entirely new vista. These are the usual rewards of travel. As I ticked off my bucket list, every new destination invariably met these expectations; the positive feelings stacked up, and the addiction took deep root. Eight years of RVing in North America served that purpose well. It was absolutely the way to do it. But now that we have had years of experience in traveling the world, somehow my views have changed.

GOING BACK TO AN OLD TIME FAVORITE

Now that I am in my seventies, I can understand what my husband has been insisting on doing for some time. Going to Mazatlan, Mexico, for example, is something he would prefer anytime over going to some new place. I asked him why, and he said, "I love the city and people. In fact, I could live there. Besides, it brings back beautiful memories." The Shrimp Capital of the World was where he took his late wife and family for vacations during the time he was steeped in a busy corporate life. I can understand why that place would bring back such joyful memories.

I agree with him that in the end it's the memories that count. And they are the ones that last. So, when you've made such memories in a place, why not go back? I have agreed to go back to Mazatlan three months a year. In fact, we have made it our third home. And

286

I do not regret it. The two of us have already been making our own special memories there.

When Bill first brought me to Mazatlan he also invited my family to be with us. We congregated for our first-ever reunion in seven years, after having all left our home in the Philippines, to celebrate my 61st birthday. We have had several reunions since then, but until today, my family considers that one the best reunion they have ever had. Bill did something so special for my family, as he did for his family before.

A trip down memory lane to a familiar destination spells comfort and convenience. You don't anxiously experience the newness of things but relive the goodness of them, even more comfortably than the first time. Each reservation, having been done before, is accomplished without mishap, very conveniently. You lean back, confident that everything will be alright and nothing will go wrong. In addition, you're able to build lasting friendships. And these are values we learn to prize more and more as we advance in years.

CHOOSING A BRAND NEW DESTINATION

Sometimes I ask, however, if I am limiting myself, foregoing chances to see more of this beautiful world, given the little time we may have left in it. But, we have taken a more pragmatic approach to travel. Honestly, the feeling of "been there, done that" calls on us more and more frequently now. How many aquariums, zoos, art museums, theme parks, beaches, mountains, etc. do we have to see to say, "We've seen enough"? So we research more, and often we are led to the conclusion: "It's nothing special." Besides, even if it is kind of special, it may be too far, too difficult to get to, or too expensive to pull off.

In fact, given all of this, we ask ourselves what other places do we truly have left on our practical bucket list? What destinations are left worth considering? An African safari, an Antarctic cruise, and an Amazonian excursion are some of what remains. But come to think of it, those journeys may, given the physical stamina they require, have already passed us by. Bill is over 76 and I am already 72. Going to such places will be extended, exhausting, and expensive.

Besides, there is more of North America that we haven't seen during our eight years of RVing. Our family reunions, both mine and Bill's, and our anniversaries are now planned around those places in the mode of travel we love best, road trips. Places like the Northeast in the glory of fall, MacKinnac Island in the splendor of summer, or the cherry blossoms of DC in spring.

There is one activity that stands out as something we absolutely must do, moreover. We are not deeply religious but, as we contemplate our mortality, the need to search for spirituality and serenity heightens. It will definitely give us peace and greater depth and, in so doing, let us learn something more about ourselves. Fatima, Lourdes, Jerusalem—one of them is definitely in the future of our next few years.

But Mexico, you are already keenly missed. We hope to see you again in a few months. Besides, there are more of you we haven't yet reached. There are 114 Magicos Pueblos and we have only been to six. In other words, I may choose an old favorite but also go to its brand new nooks and crannies. The choices are not mutually exclusive. It's not "or"; it's "and."

11

CHASING A PHOTOGRAPH

§

I used to feel that the world was at my feet. That was when I was traveling a lot for work in Manila. Nowadays I travel because my three daughters live in different cities around the world. When a daughter asks for help, I book a flight. In 2017, for the fifth time since I retired, I flew to Canada to take care of my middle daughter's three young sons in Calgary.

That gave us a chance to explore Yoho and Kootenay National Parks in British Columbia, and complete the four parks comprising the World Heritage Site of the Canadian Rockies. The third weekend included a Mother's Day getaway in Banff, a gift from my daughters. On the last weekend, I even squeezed in a visit to the new Glacier Skywalk on the Columbia Icefields between Banff and Jasper, two other national parks in Alberta we had visited before.

The only downside was that we had to drive the same section of the Trans-Canada Highway that links Calgary to the National Parks **four** times both ways. Experienced travelers do not like such a repetitive drag. Sure enough, on the road to Yoho I dozed off. Bill must have missed my chatter and nudged me: "Hey, sleepyhead, I brought you some Cheetos!" In a jiffy, the bag of my favorite cheesy snacks was almost gone. I should have been upset he'd spoiled my beauty nap. I wasn't.

Between mouthfuls, I caught a glimpse of a scene that would haunt me. A lone red car seemed to rise on the road, driving straight into an enormous glacier-draped mountain. Sadly, the image was gone in a second. "*I want that photo!*" shouted my heart. Glued to the windshield, soon I saw a second chance. Alas, the car was black, and the road was flat.

Lovely sights around Kootenay did not get my mind off that scene. The following Saturday, I was back with a vengeance. It didn't take long and another car scene appeared. The mountain was even more majestic. But the car, being white, disappeared into the mist. Again, there was no rise to the road. I cried, "Bill, can we just stage something?" Of course he dismissed my plea.

Other photo-ops were on the road. An enormous yellow truck blazoned against the grays. White clouds cavorted with snow-lined, pointed peaks. A multi-colored train ruffled through the Rockies' skirts. Cute, curvy twin bridges punctuated the highway hum-drum. Once in a while, a red-roofed cabin enlivened the greenery. Around Kootenay there was more, especially around the towns of Fields and Golden. Still, it was that striking car scene I wanted. The frustration was repeated a third time. It should have been my gift for Mother's Day, I thought.

On the last weekend the weather was itself, taking a sudden nasty turn. We proceeded and stayed at Banff for the night, hoping it would clear the next day. It didn't. But we could not go back. It was our last chance. On the way there, the coveted photo again eluded us. On the way home I kept whispering, "It's now or never."

And, just like that, it came. The car wasn't red, and low-lying clouds partly hid the mountain. But the road had a slight rise, creating the magical effect I saw the first time. Bill was so happy for me. All the way home we had a contest of who could give the best caption to the photo. Some of the entries were: "Into the Clouds", "Into the Unknown", and "Beyond the Ordinary."

Now I know. It doesn't matter how many times I have to go back to a place. It doesn't matter if I have to drive the same old familiar highway. It doesn't matter if it is not an uncommon thing I come up with. Something will catch my fancy, something will jump out of the blue, and something will be worth my while. That something was chosen by my cover designer/son-in-law for the scene behind the title in the cover of this book.

We are all free to listen to whatever our hearts whisper, even if it's just chasing a photograph.

12

EVERY TRAVELER NEEDS A GREAT TRANSPORTATION INFRASTRUCTURE

§

B orn in the slums of Manila, our family lived very near the railroad tracks that widely served Metro Manila and the largest island of Luzon. After the war, vintage jeepneys became a very popular transportation mode. Since I migrated to the US, RVed the North American continent, and traveled the world, I have come to appreciate the transportation infrastructure that makes developed countries thrive. In fact, travelers like us depend heavily on resources like the road network of America and the railway system of Europe.

The North American Road Network

I cannot tell you how much our eight years of RVing full-time in the US, Canada, and Mexico has made me appreciate the continent's road network. During that time, we traveled forty-nine American states including Alaska, nine Canadian provinces and territories, and six Mexican states. My first book *Carolina: Cruising* chronicles this epic road trip. That's when we realized that this North American road network has no equal.

Let me lift verbatim what Wikipedia says about its largest component, the US network: "The National Highway System (NHS) is a network of strategic highways within the United States, including the Interstate Highway System and other roads serving major airports, ports, rail or truck terminals, railway stations, pipeline terminals, and other strategic transport facilities. Altogether, it constitutes the largest highway system in the world." Strategically identified after WWII and officially named in 1995, today it constitutes about 165,000 miles of roads that are crucial to the country's economy, defense, and mobility. Wikipedia says it carries ninety percent of tourist traffic in the country.

This is complemented in the north by the Trans-Canada Highway, a transcontinental federal-provincial highway system that travels through all ten provinces of Canada from the Pacific Ocean in the west to the Atlantic in the east. The main route spans 4,860 miles across the country, one of the longest routes of its type in the world. This is supplemented by the 1,390-mile Alaska Highway that connects the US mainland to Alaska through Canada.

And in the south, the roadway network in Mexico also does not disappoint, especially with the   completion of parts of the concretization of Hwy 15D connecting the Mexican mainland to Arizona (and that is why we like driving to Mazatlan). The Mexican road network has 72,577 paved miles, making it the largest paved network in Latin America. Of these, 6,508 miles are multi-lane expressways, including ones with six-lanes.

With the pandemic, RVing has emerged as a preferred mode of travel. It is thus worthwhile to note that we should add to this great North American road network two other resources that make RVing a great way to explore the US. The first is the network of campgrounds, including many different kinds. They are estimated to number 4,300. The second is the availability of RV models, from the smallest teardrop trailers to the biggest luxury sixty-five-foot motorhomes. There are now estimated to be nine million RVs in the US.

But even if you do not travel North America in an RV, road trips are the best way to go from state to state or from national park to national park. The widespread availability of two other things, aside from the road network, make this mode of travel also preferred: compact cars that deliver great fuel efficiencies and the network of quality motels, hotels, AirBnBs, and home vacation rentals suited to a wide range of budgets.

NOTE: We also found the road network of Australia to be quite extensive and reliable.

THE EUROPEAN RAILWAY SYSTEM

The 2017 European Railway Performance Index ranked the performance of its national rail systems as follows:

Tier One: Switzerland, Denmark, Finland, Germany, Austria, Sweden, and France.
Tier Two: Great Britain, the Netherlands, Luxembourg, Spain, the Czech Republic, Norway, Belgium, and Italy.
Tier Three: Lithuania, Slovenia, Ireland, Hungary, Latvia, Slovakia, Poland, Portugal, Romania, and Bulgaria.

We have used all seven of the Tier One systems, six of the eight Tier Two, and three of the ten Tier Three. We especially loved our train travels from Llubijana to Bled in Slovenia, from Innsbruck to Salzburg, Vienna and back in Austria, from Oberstaufen, to Munich and Uberlinger in Germany, St. Gallen in Switzerland, Vaduz in Lichtenstein, and Paris in France, and from Paris to Brussels in Belgium. We covered all of these destinations in four weeks and a half thanks to the efficient railway system in Europe.

We tried economy and first-class trains. We tried those that served small towns and big cities. They had seamless connections with buses, taxis, and Ubers. Not a single train ride was late or canceled and we experienced no mishaps. The train stations were sometimes airport-like in the big cities, and in the smaller ones, there were quaint villages and little shops built around them as walking malls. I just love rail travel in Europe.

Bill loves it even more. He didn't have to worry about driving, and enjoyed with me the scenic views of country and city life that unfolded before us: the dwarf apple trees, the tiny garden sheds, the awesome river scenes, etc. The wide windows sometimes can even be opened for a better camera shot. We always tried the bars and dining cars, when they were available. I even found a great comfort food for my upset tummy on a train ride between Innsbruck and Vienna. Thus, we have decided that we'll no longer use rental cars on the narrow roads of Europe.

In fact we are putting together our next discovery of Europe through trains, this time in purely Tier Two and Three systems: first Spain, Portugal, Great Britain, and Ireland; and then it will be an exploration of Eastern Europe through the Czech Republic, Romania, Poland, Hungary, and Slovakia. We hope they will be as flawless and enjoyable as our past train trips. Train rides are so good for cruising past seventy.

NOTE: The metro rail systems of the big European cities also complement so well the regional and national train systems.

It is a relief that we do not have to worry about transportation wherever we go. Perhaps that is the reason why travel has exploded into the industry it is today (until, of course, it was upended by the pandemic). Road trips and the road systems have become more important today. Our cars can be as safe as we want them to be. And we don't have to travel with crowds.

13

Discovering Really Great Food

§

D uring our first all-inclusive, three-month stay in our time-share resorts in Mazatlan, Mexico we enjoyed dining in nine restaurants in four hotels featuring Mexican, Argentinian, Italian, Japanese, and International food. We could not help but think, feel, and breathe food. In fact, it has led us to make good food central to our five-country European trip in 2018.

Slovenian Cuisine

We were so lucky our friend's mother leases the ground floor of their building, just at the bottom of the trail to Ljubljana Castle, to the national Slovenian cuisine restaurant in Old Town Ljubljana. We were staying on the upper floors that comprise the B&B our friend operated. At the dinner she hosted for Bill and me, we learned about the secret to Slovenian cuisine: all natural ingredients.

Very little sugar or salt is added, because dishes depend on natural sugars and salts. In fact, most Slovenian households have small gardens in their lots where they plant their favorite vegetables and even fruit trees. In addition, water is naturally good because crystalline sources abound in the very green countryside. One thing to note: usually, dishes have no collective names. Menus list all the ingredients used instead.

Bill especially liked Slovenian sausages paired with those special buckeye wheat dumplings. But it is the cake called *prekmurska gibanica* that stole my heart. It is a layered pastry cake with fillings including poppy seeds, cottage cheese, walnuts, apples, and cream. It had just a hint of sweetness. In fact, it is common to see bees inside glass display shelves of bakeries. This dessert experience was only topped by the *kremna rezina* which another friend introduced to us when we visited him in Bled, Slovenia. It is what every tourist looks for: a vanilla pie made out of vanilla custard, whipped cream, and two very thin puff pastry layers. If you are a lover of sweets, Slovenia is definitely the place for you.

AUSTRIAN SAMPLES

As soon as we arrived in Innsbruck, we went to the grocery and found astringent persimmons in season. They were so soft, mushy, and sweet. But the next day, my stomach was a little upset. Perhaps they were over-ripe. So I starved myself until I discovered the dumplings in soup one can buy from the dining carriage as we were traveling on a train between Salzburg and Vienna. What a great comfort food. When we were in Salzburg, while Bill relished his *wiener schnitzel* at a restaurant, I again had *griesnockerlsuppe*—which I found out was what the soup dumplings are called.

Before that, Bill found a farmer's version of apple strudel at the street market in front of the Mirabell Palace and Gardens in Salzburg, where some scenes of the Sound of Music were filmed. And in Vienna, we had a sample of the famous *sacher torte*, of course. But you don't have to go in for fine dining to have good food. We had great snacks from the extra special potato slices that were being fried/grilled at the sidewalk stands. They are called *bratkartoffein*.

GERMAN FOOD

We were lucky to meet a German couple when we missed our bus at a station in Oberstaufen, Germany. They were so concerned, and "adopted" us. The next day we happened to see them again when we were checking out the RV campground. They invited us to their *maisonette* in Uberlinger, two hours away, fronting Lake Bodensee. While Bill loved all the sausages and cheeses, I always love liver *pates*. What they served us was the mildest and best-tasting I have ever had.

FRENCH STAPLES
Our most wonderful discovery in France was a kind of bread we found in the street market near our apartment at Royal Vincennes Hotel in Vincennes, a Parisian suburb. I used to love fruit cake; then I took to the German *stollen*. Now, however, I am all for the *panettone* which is actually an Italian bread. And then it was a friend from my college years who finally introduced us, after our breakfast in Laduree, the legendary restaurant near Champs Elysees, to the multi-colored and delicately sweet French macarons. They were the reason for the long lines.

BELGIAN FAVORITES
By the time we reached Belgium, the fifth country on our itinerary, we were already all out for great food. The many displays of colorful Belgian waffles with all kinds of toppings were no help. I also had a field day with lots of premium chocolates, especially the dark ones of the Leonidas variety. Bill vouches for Belgian beer, too, especially the Duvel brand, whose exclusive bar was right in front of the famous Maniekin Pis. Staff at the Visitor Center also advised us to have the best cheese fondue and beef raclette dinner at a nearby restaurant. Then, at one of the famous guild houses of the Grand Place of Belgium, we discovered beef carbonnade, beef stewed in dark Belgian ale, and *moules* soup (instead of the more popular *moules frites*).

From now on I will pay greater attention to food when we travel. It is a side of culture I had not focused on before. Now I am gung-ho about discovering classic examples of great food in a locale. They just taste so much better in the place of its origin. It also makes travel more satisfying, literally and figuratively. Besides, it is part of what we mean when we say we seek greater comfort in cruising past seventy.

14

THERE IS NO NEED
TO BREAK RULES

§

"*It's just for a photo.*" "*It's just a tiny piece.*" "*It'll just be for a second.*" Those are some excuses I told myself when I was new to this game of going from place to place.

Once we were on the Alaska Highway, just a week after starting to RV in 2009. We had just left the one-of-a-kind Signpost Forest in Watson Lake, the first big town on the legendary highway. There we bought a plank of wood, painted the words "Bill and Carol, Pittsburg, Ks/Manila, Phil. 8pm 8/8/08," and posted it in a space we could find as the 67,000th post in that "forest." After we left the town, on the way to Whitehorse—the biggest city on the Highway, between Upper Liard and Rancheria— we saw rocky embankments that had many names of people assembled from rocks found in the area.

I was still in the "leaving signs" mode, so I pleaded with Bill to stop. He did, but we found a sign that said, "Take nothing but pictures. Kill nothing but time. Leave nothing but footprints." I wondered who had put it there. Ignoring it, I started to collect rocks and began to form the letters of our names. Bill followed me. We soon realized what a time-consuming task it was and we left our opus at just two letters: B & C—not "British Columbia," not "before Christ," but "Bill and Carol."

Later I learned why the warning sign was put there. It was to prevent so many rocks being displaced that the very reason the embankment was made, to protect the road from the rushing snow/ice, would be defeated. It was early in our traveling career, so I forgave myself. It took some time before I finally really learned, however.

In fact, it was only a week later, as we were approaching Valdez, Alaska, when I broke another one. As our 24-foot Class C RV was negotiating a bend on the road, a white glistening hill loomed larger and larger. It was Worthington, a 113-acre road-accessible glacier on Richardson Highway. Bill was ecstatic, got out, and proceeded to climb the mountain of ice. I was scared. I told him, just come back with a sample of that blue ice. There I was again, foolishly breaking the travelers' golden rule again, for something that would not last anyway and just occupy space in our RV's tiny freezer.

But soon I learned, and became a better traveler. I tried hard to follow rules. Until last year, when an opportunity so irresistible presented itself. We were in Australia to babysit my youngest grandson. My daughter told us about Philip Island where the world' s littlest penguins, about a foot tall, made a nightly parade home to their burrows from a day of swimming in the ocean to feed on its bounty. And it was just a one-and-a-half hour drive from Melbourne.

We were in our seats at 4:35 pm after the walk down the long boardwalk from the Visitor Center. It was a cold night, the temperature hovering in the low 40s, but we were kind of protected where we sat so there was no wind chill. The ranger explained that the penguins wait for dark before they come in because they do not want the birds of prey to notice them. So, they wait for each other about a hundred meters from shore, and form a group for more security, before they do come in.

The previous night they had come in at 5:35 pm. They were expected to arrive at the same time. At about 5:30 pm, we were all hushed in anticipation. The excitement started to build when people spotted about two or three grouping together. They waited for more. At 5:49 pm, the group had become eight, and they bravely waddled into the space between the two viewing platforms. No photography is allowed for the Penguins' sake, but I couldn't help it. It was the cutest sight. I tried to hide the shot I took. I succeeded.

Then the ones who did not swim to feed came out of their burrows, unafraid to join those who did. They were all around the boardwalk. We walked with the penguins as we made our way up. I could not help myself and took a few more furtive shots. I was going to go on with my crime, until a ranger approached me to say, "The penguins really do not do well with the light coming from cameras." I felt so ashamed. There I was, nearing seventy, and I could not follow rules.

One thing is certain. Rules are not made to be broken. If they were, mess like the plastic trash that float on the Pacific Ocean will, sooner rather than later, gather to be such a mountain as to kill aquatic life. Rules are made for a good reason: to protect, conserve, or sustain. There's absolutely no justification for breaking them when we travel. And I direct this more to us who feel more anonymous, or more privileged, in a foreign land. But in truth, even when you are not traveling, no reason can ever be good enough to break well-formulated rules.

15

WE DARED GO TO TUNISIA

Tunisia is a name derived from its capital city, Tunis. The north-ernmost country in Africa, it has a population of about twelve million, ninety-eight percent of them Muslim. Arabic is the official language although French is also widely used. This city had often been rocked by terrorist attacks. In June 2015, for example, a gunman raided a beach hotel and killed thirty-eight people, thirty of them UK citizens, the worst terror attack against Britons in a decade. Earlier in March, the Bardo National Museum was also attacked. Twenty-two were killed. Both attacks were claimed by ISIS.

History tells us why the country is still unstable. Aside from the Greeks, the Romans, and the original Tunisians, the Arabs conquered the country in the first century of Islam. Then the Ottomans ruled for over three hundred years. The French took over in 1881, and the country finally gained her independence in 1957. It was only in 2011, however, that the Tunisian Revolution resulted in the shift to a parliamentary form of government. The only democracy in the Arab World, Tunisia is still making its difficult way to full stability.

WE SHOULD NOT HAVE GONE

My travel buddy Jingjing and I were scheduled to go to Tunisia just four months after the attack on tourists at the beach hotel. We should not have continued with our plans to go, but we had bought nonrefundable tickets. Besides, she said she knew the Filipina wife of the former Italian ambassador to Tunisia. But her friend also advised us not to go because alerts were up in most countries, the US included.

But we were fiercely stubborn. Tunisia was just the first of our four-country itinerary around the Meditteranean—in fact, we ended with seven—and we still went. I felt safer as soon as I enrolled in the US STEP program, which monitors US citizens in unstable lands. And her friend gave up dissuading us and told us to stay in the suburbs, instructing us to get in touch with their trusted former driver so he could take us around.

THE SUBURB OF SIDI BOU SAID

The expansion of the Tunisian economy in recent decades has led to the booming development of suburbs within the outer city limits. Considered a safer place, one such suburb was the lovely hilly Sidi Bou Said. It was the former home of the Said family who had converted it into a beautiful four-star hotel/bed and breakfast now called Dar Said.

I have never stayed in a lovelier place. It was authentic blue and white, traditional upper-class Muslim home. The well-crafted lobby led to the terrace with a lovely garden that overlooks the Gulf of Tunis. And each cluster of rooms was set around cute charming courtyards. Every morning there was a bountiful continental breakfast served by the pool on the terrace.

Just before you get into the group of homes on the hill that included our hotel, there is an excellent view of Tunis, Carthage and the Gulf. All the houses in the enclave had the great blue and white motif, blue windows and doors and white facades. And the narrow, winding roads were all cobbled, used by pedestrians and cars alike. One night we enjoyed couscous and lamb at the elegant restaurant just below our hotel, after going down a flight of stone steps to the bottom of the hill.

THE BARDO NATIONAL MUSEUM

Tunis has been the capital since 1159, and is the largest city of Tunisia with a population of almost three million. We did not get to see its famous Medina, a UNESCO World Heritage Site, where a tenth of its population resides and palaces, mosques, and synagogues abound. Because of the alert situation and also because it was Sunday, the only thing open was the Bardo National Museum, originally a 13th-century Hafsid palace. It is the most important archaeological museum in the Maghreb, thanks to the many discoveries in the surrounding territory. It was good the March terrorist attack didn't destroy it, because it is one of the richest Roman mosaic collections in the world, with mosaic antiquities from various periods in Tunisia's history.

THE CITY OF CARTHAGE

The Catedral de San Luis, sitting atop a hill in Carthage, can be seen from the suburbs of Tunis. It was closed, but all around it was the glory that was Rome, in expansive interior and exterior museums. Tunis had been occupied by the Berbers, but in the twelfth century BC Phoenicians started to migrate to the country and founded the city. In fact, it even rose to rival Greece, and almost destroyed Rome in the Second Punic War. It was eventually defeated in the Battle of Carthage in 149 BC. Just a few minutes away, we also visited the Thermes, the ancient baths; and then our trusted driver took us to one of the biggest mosques at the outskirts, the Sadikas glass display, and some souvenir shops.

THE RESORT TOWN OF HAMMAMET

We were also told not to miss the resort town located in the southeast of the northern peninsula called Hammamet. Many beaches make it an important tourist destination for water sports. The number of inhabitants used to quadruple to 400,000 in summer, but the recent terrorist attacks have scared away almost all the tourists except for brave or foolish souls like us.

As we made our way to Hammamet, Mount Bou Kornine kept us company. A 576-meter mountain in northern Tunisia overlooking the Gulf of Tunis, it consists of folded and faulted outcrops of Jurassic limestone. Its name comes from Tunisian Arabic meaning "the one with two horns," and that's how it looks. In ancient times, the mountain was considered sacred and rituals were conducted there.

Our trip to Tunisia ended up to be a quiet, relaxing vacation with very few tourists around. Not even a month after we left, in late November, another terrorist attack was perpetrated by ISIS. Twelve presidential guards were killed. In short, we were lucky we were there during a short window of peace. That luck was surpassed by the fact that, when I entered the photo I took of the cute courtyard leading to our room in Dar Said, it won Best of Show, Peoples' Choice, and Judges' Choice in the first ever Photo Show I ever entered. It is good we dared to go.

16

WE WERE WARNED BUT WE DROVE ANYWAY

§

"Do not go; but if you have to, fly." That was what the US State Department warned about Mazatlan, Mexico. But we were horrified that the airfare was $700 per person for just a two-hour flight. It was probably because we were going at the height of the holiday season. After calculating that we stood to save almost a thousand dollars, we decided to drive anyway. Besides, we could use a car there since we were staying for three months. In addition, we did not have to be stingy about packing. Bill could bring his golf clubs and tennis racket and I could bring back affordable and colorful treasures we find in Mexico, including bulky home décor.

THE RISK OF GOING TO MEXICO

As recently as November 4, 2019, nine members of a Mormon family, three mothers with their six children, were massacred near the town of Bavispe, Sonora, seventy miles south of the US border that was five and a half hours from where we usually stay in Hermosillo, our first stop after crossing. In fact Mazatlan, where we would eventually stay, is where the drug king El Chapo was finally arrested. Sinaloa, the state Mazatlan is in, was considered Level 4 in the US Travel Advisory, meaning "Do Not Travel," while Sonora, the state Hermosillo is in, was Level 3, "Reconsider Travel."

So I researched to find out the truth before we put ourselves in harm's way. I found the list of the 50 Most Dangerous Cities of the World in 2019, which examined those with murder rates of 35-111 per 100,000 people. The report is produced by the World Population Review. The following countries have many cities that made it to the list: Brazil, 17; Mexico, 12; Venezuela, 5; USA, 4; South Africa, 3; Honduras, 2; Colombia, 2; Jamaica, 1; El Salvador, 1; Guatemala, 1; and Puerto Rico, 1. The American cities of St. Louis (#13), Baltimore (#21), New Orleans (#44), and Detroit (#45) were all higher on the list than Mazatlan (#46). That was some source of comfort. We had been to all four during our RVing days.

Still, we continued to be nervous about our road trip. The situation at the border had deteriorated with the ongoing migrant crises at the time. So we bought male and female urinals. We figured they could be handy and would keep us from stopping at rest areas or gasoline stations unless we really had to. As for gas, we would look for the safest and newest- looking PEMEX (government) stations. If they looked ok, we could even make a rest stop there. As a further precaution, we stayed at the most expensive of the American hotel chains.

BORDER CROSSING WOES

When we approached the Mexican border at Nogales, Arizona the signs indicated "Truck Route." Since we had a car, we didn't follow the arrows. Instead, we got lost. Eventually, we found our way to the downtown border crossing called DeConcini on Grand Avenue instead of the border crossing called Mariposa on the freeway. We were happy they waved us in without any inspection. That is, until we found ourselves in the heart of downtown Nogales, Mexico. Yes, even Bill got a little concerned. People say border towns are the worst to end up in.

Later we found out that there was even a third crossing, a border station called the Morley Gate. And much later, when we were already at our Hampton Inn Hotel in Hermosillo, about three and a half hours away, we discovered that we had to go to a place called Km 21 to get tourist cards and a temporary vehicle permit for the car. The route we had taken had bypassed that point, ten kilometers past the Mariposa border crossing. Obviously, we had forgotten all these things, which we had been through during our first trip to Mazatlan in our RV ten years earlier.

It was good we were booked at our hotel for two days. So we spent our second day going back todward the Mariposa crossing, to process our paperwork at Km 21. That's where we found out we needed to put a $400 deposit on the car. We just hoped we didn't forget to get the refund on the way out or a big part of our flight savings would disappear. The beginnings of our trips are always problematic. This time, Bill had to drive seven additional hours round trip.

THE HIGHWAY TO MAZATLAN

Mexico 15D is the name of the freeway that connects Nogales, Arizona all the way to Mazatlan. From Nogales to Los Mochis, seventy percent of the highway had been changed from asphalt to concrete. It runs straight south, and our new Hyundai Elantra registered a good 44-46 mpg throughout. The toll fee collection plazas were not collecting fees anymore, but there were men and women asking for donations. We handed out an average of twenty Mexican pesos (about US $1) at about each of the eight stops on the eight-hour drive.

We stayed at Best Western Plus in Los Mochis in the northernmost tip of the Sinaloa state. In front of the hotel were the Sagrado Corazon de Jesus and a Plaza that came alive at night with many colorfully lighted kiosks that sold Mexican food. But I didn't want to risk it. We were already in Sinaloa, rated Level 4. So we had dinner at the hotel's International Restaurant. It wasn't great food, and back in the room we were further disappointed that the hotel didn't have any English channels on TV. We decided not to stay there on the way back to the US.

From Nogales to Los Mochis, the highway had been upgraded to concrete. But from Los Mochis to Mazatlan, it was as we remembered it from ten years earlier, full of potholes and Cuota Collection stops every half an hour. The fees exacted ran up to M$137 (US$7) per stop. There were eight of them on the four-hour drive. The fees were adding up but it was a good thing they still did not exact a big dent on our flight savings.

The Sinaloa state has a thriving agricultural industry. But corporations must have taken over many small farms. We saw plenty of modern farm implements that protected the plants at various stages of growth. The color of the soil they were tilling were still reddish brown, probably infused with a lot of fertilizers. But what disturbed us was the multitudes of men gathered in truck stops and in front of farm entrances hoping for farm managers to pick them up to work in the fields. Those scenes were depressing. The lack of opportunities for work was probably one of the reasons driving the drug trade.

Once we approached Mazatlan, the big blue ocean appeared to our right. It stayed with us in the last hour of our road trip. We were nervous when we started but calm slowly set in, and we were glad we had decided to drive anyway. We never got to use the urinals we had bought. And, in January next year, we plan to drive there again, especially now that we view an airplane ride as a riskier health alternative for travel.

17

TRAVEL IN THE TIME OF CORONAVIRUS

§

On January 21, 2020 it was reported that the coronavirus ravaging China had arrived in the US, in Seattle, Washington. We were on our annual three-month, all-inclusive vacation at a resort in Mazatlan, Mexico. Naturally, I worried since the most vulnerable was reported to be older people, like Bill and me, especially those with compromised immune systems.

CUTTING SHORT OUR MEXICAN VACATION

We had inserted a two-week Puerto Vallarta trip into our Mazatlan stay. On March 11, when we were on the second week, the WHO officially declared COVID-19, the coronavirus disease, a pandemic. We did not want to cut short our stay, so we practiced social distancing: we did not join tours, visited landmarks at non-peak times, went to outdoorsy places, and tried to keep the required healthy distance from the people we found in the places we visited.

When we got back to Mazatlan on March 14, Europe had become the new epicenter, and panic-buying in the US had set in. We had twelve more scheduled days in Mexico but we decided to cut short our stay and canceled our tours to La Noria, La Concordia, and San Carlos. Then we shopped for staples, including toilet paper, alcohol wipes, and cleaners at Walmart and local grocery chain Soriana.

The statistics were pretty grim when we left Mexico. The US had become the new epicenter, and the Canadian and Mexican borders had been closed to non-essential travel. It took us two days, driving eight hours each day, to get home. What was surprising was it took us no time at all at the Mariposa Border on both the Mexico and US sides. There was not the usual inspection done. But what was scary was that there was no Covid testing done.

But home is the best place to do self-isolation, not on a cruise ship out at sea or a hotel room in a foreign country. We had completed our fourteen-day period of self-isolation when the local authorities declared a lockdown to the end of April. I wouldn't say it was welcome news, but it was not a problem. There were a few things we have learned to do to make it a more meaningful pause.

CREATIVE IDEAS IN LOCKDOWNS

The new normal was beginning to be shaped by things like online shopping, grocery pick-ups, ingredient substitutions in cooking, exercising with videos, new levels of cleaning, and movies on demand. Zoom participation also exploded, fostering online activities that replaced physical interactions. And then, as before, I found some projects that made the time more productive.

Utilizing technology to keep engaged with family and friends was normal for us while we were RVing. It was no different during the time of coronavirus. Since all of my daughters and sons-in-law were busy working from home or being essential workers who go to work, I thought it best to help with the kids. I conducted an hour-long session three times a week with my grandsons, ages four to six, and another once a week with those ages thirteen to fourteen. I was so happy that I got more engaged with my family. I even upgraded my Zoom to "pro" to enable longer meetings—the free version is maxed at 40 minutes—and to launch Zoom parties for residents of Viewpoint, featuring online bingo and trivial pursuit. We also had regular Zoom meetings, parties, and fundraisers with my national and state alumni associations. And, as a matter of fact, it will be used heavily during the marketing of this book.

As before, whenever there is a problem, I always turn to some project on which I can focus my full attention. The last time, when Bill and I stayed apart, my first book *Carolina: Cruising* was born. This time, during the Covid-19 lockdown, I was able to write this book (but I did not change the title to *Cruising with Coronavirus*). This is what I call a flagship project, the kind big enough to consume one's energy, fueled by one's passion. Finding a flagship project can be a great antidote to an over-arching problem. Your attention is absorbed by something worthy of your time.

NEW WAYS OF TRAVELING

But, with a traveler's soul, we had to find ways to continue encountering fresh places and ideas. As soon as the lockdown was lifted, we considered our car an extension of our home; it is a place we keep as clean as we can. We created a short list of places where we could go, breathe good fresh air, and practice natural social distancing, like the state, regional, and national parks around us that were still open. When we didn't see people on the trails, we got out of the car and walked a little. If not, we just continued driving. The operative principle was to distance ourselves from others, but not from nature.

In fact, when there was a resurgence of coronavirus cases in Arizona, we decided that we should actually go from our higher risk home to lower risk areas that accepted us. We went to three mountain retreats in Utah, Colorado, and California, and invited our children to meet with us there. But since they were not in our bubble—the people you live with and share daily activities with, like Bill and I are for each other—we developed certain rules to follow when we were with them. Those rules followed the principles of avoiding crowds, social distancing, preferring the outdoors, frequent hand washing, and the wearing of masks (details are provided in the next chapter, "On Keeping Fit").

We canceled our trips in April but resumed our travels in July. And we still intend to go to Mexico for our annual stay in January, if conditions continue to improve and therapeutics and vaccines advance. Self-isolation helped flatten the curve for our community and the world when we had to do it. Creative ideas helped us remain productive during the lockdown. And with new rules, we have found a way to continue traveling and still be safe.

18

ON KEEPING FIT

§

That brings us to the most crucial topic for cruising past seventy. Keeping fit includes the matters of exercise, food intake, and healthcare. We had to keep fit before; but now we have to focus on more if we want to travel better and longer. So I have added the new matter that is of utmost important today: how we interact with others.

Cardiovascular issues plague Bill. My issues are hypothyroidism, and nagging gastrointestina and other-stress-related problems like hypertension. They started when we were full-time RVing and we didn't pay enough attention to healthcare. Mesmerized by America's beauty, we were always eager to see everything, always on the go. I am glad we have slowed down. Now we can focus on these.

REGULAR EXERCISE

Back in Seattle before our cruising days, we went to Bally's and then LA Fitness (the chain that bought the former) three times a week. When we went on our five-year cross-continent runs in RVs, however, the fitness facilities in campgrounds were not consistent. We thought hiking would be our main exercise regimen. But when hordes of mosquitoes feasted on us, the habit did not take root. At other times, it was either too cold or too hot. And even if sight-seeing meant walking a lot, it didn't resemble exercise. It was more leisurely strolling.

We thought there must be a way of keeping fit through exercise even while we are on the go. I dreaded the thought that we were slipping quietly into the sedentary habits of seniors. But I rational-ized that we had just not yet formed good exercise habits because we were still in transition. When it was already way past transition time, we had to resolve to do at least two of the following or suffer health consequences:

1. Find the time to play a sport for at least an hour three times a week (table tennis, billiards, mini-golf, badminton, golf, tennis, pickle ball or dance). I choose to dance. It is actually easier now, with "We Love Dance" videos.
2. If there's a gym, exercise for at least an hour, three times a week. If there is none, exercise in your own home using vid-eos. I chose a gym pre-coronavirus. Now, I stick to the Jenny McLendon for Seniors You Tube channel.
3. Walk for an hour before nightfall at least three times a week, if you haven't walked enough during the day. Bill needs to walk. And he can drag me with him. I allow him to do that once in a while, especially in naturally socially distanced parks.

HEALTHY FOOD INTAKE

When we were doing a lot of driving in the RV and car, we would cut up a lot of veggies and fruits and have nuts available for snacks, with lots of water to wash them down. When we settled at campgrounds longer, nesting in a bigger RV, we began to cook more meals. This tendency worsened when we settled in Viewpoint, where I had a larger kitchen. When we started to love local cuisine, it led to hearty eating. The worst was in Mexico, when we were in an all-inclusive resort. We needed to resolve to do the following as an eating regimen:

1. Eat one big meal a day, preferably lunch, and two other small ones; or just two regular meals, late breakfast and early dinner. Stick to vegetable dishes beyond salads. I choose to stick to three meals. And I now have twenty great vegetable dishes from around the world.

2. "Graze" throughout the day with light morning, afternoon and evening snacks, preferably fruits or nuts. This one is very easy for me. As a treat for these darker times, however, we have added favorite cookies, but only a maximum of two a day, one each as dessert for lunch and dinner.

3. Eat out infrequently, only for a special occasion or celebration. Compensate with smaller meals the rest of the day when you do. Covid-19 locked in this habit. When we do eat out, it has to be either a curbside pick-up or patio seating.

In addition, we adopted two novel ways of skipping a meal twice a week. One was by going to a movie during lunch time and sticking to one large popcorn bag, which we shared. Also, Costco's food samples substitute for lunch or dinner when we shop for supplies. These two had become a regular part of our program, until coronavirus struck. So, now we skip the popcorn while watching movies on demand and skip going to Costco (they have suspended giving samples).

After our RVing phase, we now stick to staying in our time-share units. Their kitchens allow us to have fun at local groceries, buying lots of goodies we don't find in stores back home, and learning how to cook exciting local fare (and whenever we miss them, our usual favorites). With the threat of coronavirus, we have also found that timeshares treat us like homeowners, reserving a minimum of twelve hours between check-in and check-out of guests and not allowing anyone else to come in our rooms during our entire stay.

Beginning January 2019, however, we started to have twelve weeks of all-inclusive stays in Mexico. We went wild during our first year. I added some pounds and a belly bump. But, in our second year, we learned to fill our plates from the abundant selection of veggies (artichokes, hearts of palm, Brussel sprouts included) and fruits, especially since they are mostly the tropical ones I miss most in Arizona (papayas, avocadoes, mangoes).

But we still need to rump up our resolve. We are glad the steaks are not that good in Mexico so we stick to seafood and chicken. But we can't eliminate dessert and have learned to share one instead. We rationalized that we can't give up all the little pampering we feel entitled to at this age, like the two cookies we each have allowed to complete our day.

PREVENTIVE HEALTH CARE

As we have shown, the main drawback of the full-time RVing lifestyle was the lack of regular preventive health care. Settling in Phoenix was the smartest decision we ever made. There is excellent geriatric care, with the high population of snowbirds. We found an excellent family doctor who keeps track of regular screening and refers us to the best of specialists. Diagnosed with two conditions

CAROLINA ESGUERRA COLBORN

(early hypothyroidism and early hypertension), I was brought back to normal with half the smallest dosages of the required meds. Meanwhile, Bill has been fitted with a pacemaker and is seen every four months for the skin melanoma he had developed.

INTERACTING WITH OTHERS

And, as I mentioned in the previous chapter, we have developed new rules for keeping safe during this time. They follow the principles of avoiding crowds, social distancing, and preferring the outdoors, in addition to frequent hand washing and the wearing of masks, especially when interacting with others that don't belong to our bubble. For the foreseeable future, especially when we are still under the threat of viral diseases, we will follow these practices, especially numbers one to five. We still hope these rules can be relaxed later; but the sixth we hope we can do away with sooner, especially with loved ones.

1. Go to areas with lower incidences of Covid-19. It is good that there are plenty of data to drill down to, even to zip codes. We have selected restaurants, groceries, mountain retreats, towns, counties, and states, this way.

2. Meet only in uncrowded open-air spaces. Stick to patio seating for eating out, drive-in theaters for watching movies, outdoor services for worship, and hiking at off-the-beaten-path trails as a preferred activity.

3. Do not spend unreasonably long time with others. CDC says more than fifteen minutes is too long. But, as long as we are socially distanced and masked, we have extended this to a maximum of two hours.

4. Do not ride with others in the same vehicle. This makes us stick to our car as our preferred mode of travel. We are currently eliminating planes, ships, trains, and buses as options for travel.
5. Do not share rooms with people not in your bubble. So we no longer stay in our children's homes and no longer book multi-bedroom units but keep to separate units if we meet in hotels or resorts. We also stick to our timeshares. As owners, we feel better taken care of.
6. Do not shake hands or hug. When we cannot help it and want to express some warmth, we elbow-bump for a second.

With regular exercise, healthy food intake, preventive health care, and safer ways of interacting with others, we look forward to being fit and to more years of traveling, past seventy.

CONCLUSION

§

SHIFTING MY APPROACH TO TRAVEL
Note: This section was written for and published by *TravelAwaits*.

We are definitely now traveling more in keeping with our age. It has been a decidedly welcome shift. When we were in our sixties, we were bouncing around. Bill and I had just married, we plunged into RVing, and it seemed to be a never-ending honeymoon. I drove my husband nuts, because I wanted to see so many things and felt we had so little time. As I approached and reached my seventies, the purpose, pace, and budget of our travels changed.

PURPOSE
When I became a sexygenarian, I was already retired. I opted for early retirement because work had burned me out by the time I reached the age of 54. I traveled for work, but I usually just saw the four walls of a hotel since I was too focused on earning enough as a single parent. Thus, when I retired, I felt my time had finally come. I wanted to see as much of the world as possible.

One story I will never forget happened when I was 61, I had stayed up all night to wait for the Northern Lights in Dawson City in Canada's Yukon, but had been terribly disappointed. Instead of going back down to mainland USA, I urged Bill to drive farther north to the Arctic Circle. We spent three days and two nights on a dirt gravel road. Our RV almost died had my husband not used his belt to prop up the tail pipe that had broken loose.

Even before I reached my seventies, however, things had begun to change. Bill says the turning point probably came when we started to hibernate during winter at Viewpoint. Our momentum was broken, and inertia set in. He discovered he was already tired of hooking and unhooking the RV every two to three weeks. It was time to slow down, he said. Bill had already turned seventy, so it was understandable. Only four years younger, pretty soon I followed his lead.

We bought a home base at Viewpoint and sold our motorhome. We were finally able to make a real home, eight years after we married. Our traveling lifestyle changed. Now we search for comfortable places where family and friends can stay together, where we have can relive great memories, or where our timeshare memberships have a great resort for us to enjoy. We intend to explore the areas around these temporary "homes" as comfortable bases.

PACE

The two decades also couldn't be farther apart in terms of pace. In my sixties, I was obsessed with speed. In the beginning we stayed only three to four days at a campground. Later our stays became longer, but only to a maximum of two or three weeks. I felt I had the energy of a fifty-year-old. But, having reached my seventies, I have changed.

When I was sixty-nine, for example, I traveled to four Southeast Asian countries in just four days with my girlfriends. Now that I am seventy-two, I have begun to see things Bill's way. We have started to like spending rest time at a base, like at home, and use it to explore the neighboring areas with more comfort and convenience. I have started to see the wisdom of the slow and gradual revelation of landscapes, landmarks, and stories around us wherever we are.

Last March—before our trip was cut short by the pandemic—Bill and I spent two weeks in Puerto Vallarta, Mexico instead of our usual week. After a busy day trip, we took a rest day at the beautiful beach behind our resort in Nuevo Vallarta before doing another trip the following day. We were able to cover all the places we wanted to see and still had time to luxuriate at the resort, the nearby marina, and the diverse restaurants in the neighborhood.

BUDGET

When we were in our sixties, we bought second-hand RVs, cooked most of our meals, and delighted at finding treasures in Goodwill Stores. Our income had shrunk to the monthly pension from Social Security, investment dividends, and rental money from our homes. We were so successful in following our budget that we lived on far less than when we stayed at home, while we were RVing.

When I was sixty-nine I flew thirty-six hours from Phoenix to Melbourne instead of the normal eighteen because the fare that included long layovers in Guangzhou was dirt cheap. Well, I never got to see the city like I'd hoped in supposed quick day trips. Instead I suffered in the airport for seven hours on the way there and twelve hours on the way back, both times without Facebook! In addition, we regularly chose cheaper lodging even if it was far from the city center. And there were many times we chose street or fast food to save on travel dollars.

Now that Bill and I are in our seventies, we feel the need to travel more comfortably, if not stylishly. Being older, we look for more conveniences. That usually means a higher budget, which in turn leads to traveling more selectively. It's good our children told us it was ok for us to die poor. Now we are vacationing in time-shares that give us a consistent level of quality, sometimes luxury, at a more reasonable cost.

When we were in Mougins, France for a week for example, we realized we didn't have enough time to cover all the places we wanted to see. So we rented a car with a driver to take us to all the picturesque towns around the French Riviera, including the small towns of Ese, St. Paul de Vence, and Grasse. The same car and driver took us to Monaco, too. Maybe later on, we will even not mind upgrading to business, or even first class, for long haul flights.

Now I can say that I am past bouncing around. I prefer slow and immersive travels. We look for a base where we can stay prefer-ably for a minimum of two weeks and from where we can leisurely explore the neighboring areas with comfort and convenience. Our all-inclusive three-month stay at a resort in Mexico will be a main-stay, too. In other words, going to every country is no longer a dream.

CRUISING TO THE END

This book was my flagship project when we were on relative self-isolation in Arizona. True, I was able to make a few trips to state and regional parks that were left open and some surprising small towns of character we found along the way. True, we were also able to go to lower risk areas, retreat to the mountains, and be with some family. But it was also the time I thought about how it will be if I truly cannot travel anymore.

When Phoenix became the new hotspot after New York's ordeal subsided, a feeling of hopelessness set in. And then my mind took me to musing about the seven years still remaining in my seventies, how I will travel in my eighties, even my nineties. But, even as I am getting ready for the time when, not if, the relative self-isolation will be lifted and we can travel freely again, my thoughts always return to the same question. I wonder if, and when, I will end up not being able to travel any longer.

Our travels have steadily become less, from twelve months to eight in my sixties, to six in my seventies. It will probably reduce further to four in my eighties and may just be two in my nineties. At the end of this decade, we will probably change the way we travel again, as we did at the end of my sixties. We will probably spend more months at home in Phoenix, staying home even in the hot days of summer or the cold days of winter. And we may probably end up limiting our travels mainly to spending our customary three months in Mexico. Maybe that will even decline to two, and later one.

Since by then we should also have probably exhausted all the day trips possible here in Phoenix and there in Mexico, stays in both bases will not really be travels but just become time at home. Even our summers will change from extended road trips to visit family and friends. Instead, we may see them in just two weeks of reunions, one with Bill's family and another with mine, at selected timeshare locations. We are hoping that they will visit us more at Viewpoint, though. And we are already in the process of adding a spacious Arizona room for that purpose.

Another most probable scenario is a regular vacation in Sedona, the beautiful red rocks city, or Flagstaff, that refreshing mountain city, which are both at higher elevations and much cooler than and only two or two and a half hours from Phoenix. We will probably also no longer be able to travel to the Philippines and Australia, unless we fly business or first-class, and only for significant family events, when it is safe to do so. My youngest daughter makes Melbourne, Australia her home and I still have two sisters in Manila.

My writing will also probably change. In my seventies, I added inner journeys to my travel diaries, like what you have in this book. As I approach my eighties, because we will be going to fewer new places, I will probably be shifting to musings about life in general, albeit in different settings. And the theme will probably shift to "Cruising to the End," unless I can find a better title. I hope there will still be energy for that third "cruising" book.

And this is when I begin to feel very positive. Even if my outer journeys will gradually decrease to almost nothing, there will be even more inner journeys. And I will continue to write about both, hoping to inspire those of you who discovered travel late in life because you see it is indeed quite possible, and those of you who are starting it early because you see that it can be a way of life.

Even if we are traveling less we can look back at past trips, and look forward to future ones. And, from every trip we make, let us build our books of lessons learned, changes made, and insights gained. The secret has been and will always be simple. Do not deny your traveler's soul. Let it roam free. And eat lots of chicken wings and, if possible, also chicken feet.

ACKNOWLEDGMENTS

$$\int$$

"The only people who truly know your story are the ones that helped you write it."

It's too bad we do not know who wrote this insightful sentence. I love it because I believe it to be true. As a writer, I know for a fact that there are many other people without whom the episodes could never have even happened (at worst) or could not have happened as they did (at best). And there are those without whom my words and pictures could have been inadequate to tell them.

First, as I mentioned in the Preface, there were six people whose views influenced the final shape of this book. They are dear, dear friends and fellow travelers from Viewpoint, El Cid, and even family of loved ones. Meticulously reading either the first or second drafts, they gave me copious feedback in a developmental edit that led to the major restructuring, rewriting, and redoing of the original draft:

1. First manuscript: Carol Chamberlain, Sue Shuckhart, and Gary Townsend
2. Second manuscript: Rita Taylor, Lily Beth Brazones, and Bill Pallucca

Second, I cite in particular Gary Townsend, who is considered Viewpoint's Resident Editor. We both got together regularly with authors in the park, trying to improve our craft. He pored over every single word, punctuation mark, and format, leaving a great number of red ink "chicken tracks" on the pieces of paper. I just hope I was able to faithfully execute every improvement.

Third, I would like to thank Don Robertson, author of eight Western best-sellers, and his wife Paula who helped me navigate publishing through Kindle. The great thing is that, like Gary and Sue above, they also are dear neighbors in Viewpoint.

Fourth, I am so indebted to my artist son-in-law Deejay Aberion who worked with me in developing a highly creative and charming cover for my book. A good cover is so crucial to a successful book and he delivered three that were submitted to a Facebook poll. Almost four hundred people participated and chose the cover.

Of course, I would also like to thank all of those who actually had starring roles in this travel story.

First and foremost is my husband Bill. If we did not get married, I would not have lived the best part of my life. He single-handedly hooked and unhooked, drove and parked, and drained and filled up the RV. And even after that, I would depend on him for every little movement at train stations, airports, and bus depots. My life of travel would never have been born or lived without him. And, even with my writing, he was always the first editor of any post or article I produce! It is as if, if he didn't say "go ahead" with it, I wouldn't.

And then there is my beloved family, my daughters Trisha, Claudine, and April, together with my sons-in-law Deejay, Arnold, and Clint. They not only brought me to so many new places and adventures but also brought me the most precious memories with my grandchildren, Krishna, Daniela, Kenji, Enzo, Kai, Jax, and

Kyrie. There are my sisters and their families, Bill's sister and her family, and his children and grandchildren. They were all part of our support system.

And, of course, there are my friends. There are those who came with me on some of my travels when Bill could not. There are those whom I met in my trips, and there are those who were waiting for us when we came back. There are those whom we visited, and those who visited us. Many helped promote this book through social media because it was the only way I could get the word out during these trying times. Again there was Jingjing who helped me with mainstream media, blogs, and podcasts. And there are all those who are in, around, and between all the lines of this book. Thank you all.

ABOUT THE AUTHOR

§

C arolina Esguerra Colborn had a distinguished career in Philippine business
before retiring early at 54, and migrating to
the US in 2004. She was former President/
CEO of BayanTrade, e-procurement hub
of the Philippines; Managing Director of
SAP Philippines; Deputy Commissioner of
the Bureau of Internal Revenue; General
Manager of MegaLink, the ATM trans-
action switch of banks, and Vice-President of the Development
Academy of the Philippines, the government consulting arm. She
also worked for Andersen Consulting, IBM and NCR. Twice a recip-
ient of the Most Powerful Women in IT Award, she represented the
private sector in the National Information Technology Council.

Carolina settled in Seattle, Washington where her eldest daughter lived. While babysitting a grandson, she also taught as adjunct
professor in business at Seattle Central Community College, Central
Washington University, and Renton Technical College. She even
volunteered at SCORE, the Service Corps of Retired Executives, as
a small business counselor and lecturer on marketing.

In 2007, she met Bill and they married a year later. Soon he sold
his business, and they embarked on an eight-year cruise of North

America in RVs. In 2015 this epic journey was chronicled in her first travel book, *Carolina: Cruising to an American Dream*. She has also released a handy booklet, *Cruising in an RV: the basics you need to know*, for those looking to start RVing. Because she had time during the 2020 lockdown, this was followed by a collection of the best-loved and most widely-read posts on her blog, *Cruising Past 70*. The book, *Cruising Past Seventy. It's Not Only about Outer Journeys. It's Also about Inner Ones.*, focuses on inner journeys that arise from outer ones in three themes of lessons learned, changes made, and insights gained.

Carolina also writes bimonthly for *TravelAwaits*, an online travel magazine. She and her husband now use Phoenix, Arizona as a base for their travels. She has traveled to forty-eight countries. She holds a BS in Math, MBA, and DPA abd from the University of the Philippines.

Email Address:	carol.colborn@gmail.com
Blog:	https://rvcruisinglifestyle.blogspot.com
Website:	https://www.carolcolborn.wix.com/carolinacruising
Facebook Personal Page	https://www.facebook.com/carolesguerracolborn/
Facebook Business Page	https://www.facebook.com/cruisinglifestylebookseries/
Twitter	https://twitter.com/carolcruising/
LinkedIn	https://www.linkedin.com/in/carolesguerracolborn/
Pinterest	https://www.pinterest.com/CarolinaCruising/
Travel Awaits	https://www.travelawaits.com/author/carol-colborn/

Made in the USA
Monee, IL
05 November 2023

45818657R00204